ACCELERATE
Your
IMPACT

ADAPTIVE FINANCIAL PLANNING
FOR TODAY'S ECONOMY

JASON INGRAM

Introduction by Jonathan Krueger

Copyright © 2021 by LionsGate Advisors.

All rights reserved. No part of this book may be reproduced in any written, electronic, recording, or photocopying without written permission of the publisher or author. The exception would be in the case of brief quotations embodied in articles or reviews and pages where permission is specifically granted by the publisher or author.

LionsGate Advisors
14755 North Outer Forty Rd. Suite 415
Chesterfield, MO 63017
Printed in the United States of America

Although every precaution has been taken to verify the accuracy of the information contained herein, the author and publisher assume no responsibility for any errors or omissions. No liability is assumed for damages that may result from the use of information contained within.

Accelerate Your Impact/ Jason Ingram & Jonathan Krueger -- 1st ed.

CONTENTS

Foreword ix

Preface 1

Introduction BY Jonathan Krueger, CEO, LionsGate Advisors 5

Section I: How Did We Get Here?

Chapter 1 The Lion and the Gazelle 9

Chapter 2 Now What? 19

Chapter 3 2020 - 2029 & Beyond Economic Forecast 21

Chapter 4 It's Just MATH 29

Chapter 5 Aging Population A Demographic Time-bomb 35

Chapter 6 What's Wrong with This… 47

Chapter 7 No Gold Watches 51

Section II: Purpose, Plan, Progress

Chapter 8 The Process 67

Chapter 9 Accelerating the Impact of Your Wealth 91

Chapter 10 Replacing the Bond Position 107

Chapter 11 Tax-Free Investments in Your Portfolio 129

Chapter 12 How to Utilize the Market in Your Retirement Portfolio Income is What Matters… 143

Section III: The Third Act

Chapter 13 When to Take Social Security 153

Chapter 14 Live, Quit, or Die An Honest Conversation about Extended Care 165

Chapter 15 The Family Office 185

Chapter 16 Secure Estate and Legacy Planning 191

Chapter 17 It Depends 199

Funding Life Insurance as a Contingent Asset Class in a Balanced Portfolio by Jonathan Krueger 207

Appendix 221

The Secures Act: What Does It Mean For You? 223

Footnotes for The Secure Act 229

Disclosure 231

"If anyone can do it, you can." In the darkest hours and when I feared I might not succeed she was there with the greatest encouragement of all. To my late dear mother, Alma Mae, whose guidance and belief in me and my abilities never faltered, even once. She was truly the personification of Agape Love: Love, expecting nothing in return.

She is the Gazelle in the "Lion and the Gazelle" story. That short verse was on the wall of her sewing room; it now hangs in my office, and she knew absolutely that when the sun comes up, you'd better be running.

We're doin' it, Alma!!

DISCLAIMER:

This content is for informational purposes only. The reader should not construe any such information or other material as legal, tax, investment, financial or other advice. Nothing contained in this book constitutes a solicitation, recommendation, endorsement or offer by the authors, LionsGate Advisors or any third-party service provider to buy or sell any securities or other financial instruments in any other jurisdiction in which such solicitation or offer would be unlawful under the securities laws of such jurisdiction.

All content in this book is information of a general nature and does not address the circumstances of any particular individual or entity. Nothing in this book constitutes professional and/or financial advice, nor does any information on the site constitute a comprehensive or complete statement of the matters discussed or the law relating thereto. Neither the authors nor LionsGate Advisors is a fiduciary by virtue of any person's use of or access to the content herein. You alone assume the sole responsibility of evaluating the merits and risks associated with the use of any information or content contained herein before making any decisions based on such information or content.

There are risks associated with investing in securities. Investing in stocks, bonds, exchange traded funds, mutual funds and money market funds involves risk of loss. Loss of principal is possible. Some high-risk investments may use leverage, which will accentuate gains & losses. Foreign investing involves special risks, including a greater volatility and political, economic and currency risks and differences in accounting methods. A security's or a firm's past investment performance is not a guarantee or predictor of future investment performance.

FOREWORD

Retirement

In little more than a century, retirement has advanced in complexity and requires careful planning. In 1960, the average man lived to the age of 66.6 years. Today, an average American male has a life expectancy of 78.93 years, almost a decade longer! In 2100 (for someone born today, approximately), average life expectancy is predicted to be 88.78 years, meaning another decade of life and, therefore, another decade of retirement to fund.

My career has spanned 36 years in the retirement business. I have built and managed companies that have served over 500,000 pre-retirees or retirees planning for a safer, more predictable retirement. Investors have entrusted us with over $50 billion in retirement assets. I do not take this responsibility lightly.

What I have learned from this is experience is simple. American retirement needs are simple. Retirees are searching for retirement income that is dependable and secure. They want to better manage taxes before and during retirement. Most importantly—they seek to protect the principal that represents a lifetime of work and gratification forgone.

For some, it is the culmination of a lifetime of dreams. For others, it is financial fear and dread. Regardless of circumstance, retirement is in a category unto itself. A thousand—or thousands of—small decisions regarding saving and deferring gratification are the cornerstone. Working, saving, spending, and career moves are all critical. Without lifestyle behavioral decisions during our earning years, there will be few assets upon which to retire.

Overwhelmingly, Americans also seek help—professional, experienced, thoughtful advice. The investment advice is not necessarily confusing, but to the retired engineer, small business owner, teacher—or really any of us—they are not in our profession's language. Therefore, help can be the difference between a comfortable retirement and a stressful retirement.

Jason Ingram is one of these professionals, one whose knowledge and experience can help educate investors and lay out a course through the complexity and confusion of investing. He has the knowledge and expertise to allow retirees to sleep soundly and without fear.

Benjamin Franklin said, "If you fail to plan, then you plan to fail."

This is as true today as it was over 250 years ago. This is the heart of Jason's message, to plan. Comfortable retirement cannot be accomplished without a plan—and Jason's core principle is to help investors build a plan unique to each of his clients and manage the plan from the beginning through all of life's complex needs. What elevates Jason above so many excellent financial advisors is his capability to distill a lifetime of financial planning experience into a comprehensive and coherent guide.

Most investors are not prepared for a retirement that can sometimes equal the entirety of a working life. They are also not ready for the course corrections required of an unpredictable set of markets. We can rely upon a professional like Jason to understand the markets, the tax code and customizing a portfolio to an individual's risk tolerance.

I hope you enjoy this book as much as I have. Remember, APPLIED knowledge is power!

Take heed. Engage a professional. Make a plan. Follow the plan. Enjoy your retirement.

Wade A. Dokken

President, Wealthvest

Co-founder of WealthVest, a comprehensive financial services sales, marketing and distribution company and the largest independently owned distributor of fixed and index annuities to banks and broker-dealers. Wealthvest is headquartered in Bozeman, Montana, with offices in San Francisco, California.

PREFACE

I am frequently awed by the people I meet. It might be sitting at the table with a recently or soon-to-be retired family or introducing myself to a small class of adult learners at one of the colleges where I teach. Regardless of the setting, I marvel and am amazed as they outline their dreams for the future and how they got to where they are today, financially and spiritually.

Most of them are planners, or so they believe. In their respective fields as engineers, pilots, physicians, educators, or executives, they have prepared for their futures, and done so successfully. That's what brought them to either my classroom or our offices. They are smart, hungry and humble for the most part. They're pretty sure they've done everything right, but they're aware that there may be holes in their financial knowledge. That's why we find ourselves together; this professional wants to know what they don't know and they want to know it TODAY! What an admirable position to be in: looking forward to a great stress-free retirement.

This book, my second in financial education, came about because I see myself as a educator first, and a financial planner second. With a "teach a man to fish" mentality, I love it when someone gets it. For instance, my team was working with an engineer client, teaching her how to use a very complicated spreadsheet. Though she has spent her life in spreadsheets, this one was tricky, but the moment her face lit up with that look of, "Oh! Now I get it!" is one I remember well. Likewise, the relief that smoothed over the worry lines of an educator when he realized he would not have to worry about having enough for his retirement. That fills my cup. My eyes twinkle when I see the couple who want to not only take care of their families after they're gone but have a hunger to give more now. They want to pay it forward. Those stories are my purpose and my why.

The objective of this book is to educate.

I began this book in the fall of 2019 and could never have begun to imagine how the world would change by the time I wrote this preface.

I believed the markets were over-inflated and the economy was being propped up. I believed we were in for a correction at least in the markets, and I firmly believed we were/are on an unsustainable spending spree and Congress has continued to kick the can down the road on repayment. I feared for the future of our great country and my children and grands. Where would the buck stop?

We now find ourselves in an unfathomable pandemic. At this point, no one really knows how long it will go on, nor how it will impact us all now or in one year or two. It is truly uncharted territory.

The new reality of limited travel, economic adjustments, and possible world recession or depression is real, as is the effect of the unknown on markets and individuals. I now view the world quite differently; there was the time before COVID-19 and after. Where we are now, this murky confusing time of masks and rolling closures, that's the great unknown, isn't it?

In writing this book, I have researched a number of expert sources to complement my own perspective. I have looked to the inspirational works of Tony Robbins at times and to the Congressional Budget Office at other times. It is truly a compilation.

While none of us truly knows the motivation of any political party, politician, economist, or scientist, the premise of much of this book falls on the pioneers of math: Archimedes, Newton, and Einstein. I do not judge nor favor any political party over the other. My motivation in calling out either the Democrats or the Republicans is to just help you to see. It doesn't matter who holds the power, it only matters that you, the reader, are educated about how math works in our fiscal structure. Lest the mention of complicated calculations should deter you, let me say this: Fear Not the Math! This book is here to assist you in preparing your ship for the ocean voyage of retirement.

And, yes, it is a voyage. The winds will change, the currents will bend and move you, and the weather will affect your journey.

"In ancient times, mariners depended on the Polaris, the North Star, to find their latitude on the voyage. At the North Pole, Polaris is directly overhead at 90 degrees. At the equator, which is zero degrees latitude, Polaris is on the horizon with zero degrees altitude. Between the equator and the North Pole, the angle of Polaris above the horizon is a direct measure of terrestrial latitude.

In the ancient world, the navigator who was planning to sail out of sight of land would measure the altitude of Polaris as he left home port (today's latitude). To return after his long voyage, he needed to only sail north or south, as appropriate, to bring Polaris to the altitude of the home port, then turn left or right as appropriate and 'sail down the latitude,' keeping Polaris at a constant angle" (Peter Ifland, Curator of the Physics Museum at the University of Coimbra).

The astrolabe, the quadrant and the sextant were tools developed to make these measurements of latitude more accurate. Over the course of time, those rudimentary tools evolved to today's sophisticated satellite navigations systems that are accurate to within a few feet.

Math was the driving force behind it all.

I hope this book will serve you well as you navigate the tricky waters of retirement. Grandchildren, travel, and your next book to read should be your worry, not, *will my money run out* or *what if I get ill?*

Safe sailing, and may the wind be always at your back, the seas calm, and the sunsets captivating.

Crossing the Bar - Alfred, Lord Tennyson
"Twilight and evening bell,
And after that the dark!
And may there be no sadness of farewell,
When I embark;
For tho' from out our bourne of Time and Place
The flood may bear me far,
I hope to see my Pilot face to face
When I have crossed the bar."

INTRODUCTION

BY JONATHAN KRUEGER, CEO, LIONSGATE ADVISORS

It's rare to see two people with opposing political beliefs collaborate effectively in business, but Jason and I are living proof that it can be done. Like anything else, success in business and in life requires a commitment to sharing a belief, drive, and an element that Tony Robbins calls "CANI," a constant and never-ending improvement. While Jason and I may disagree on about 98% of everything politically, we have found a common ground in two unwavering truths. First, we both view business as ministry. Second is our shared concern in the financial well-being of our country.

Today's financial planning requires more than just theoretical assumptions and past performance analysis; it requires a keen sense of awareness of the potential disrupters that could sabotage your ability to create, keep, and maintain wealth.

In this book, Jason outlines the concerns that we both believe could disrupt your ability to build and retain savings. Jason dedicates much of his time to teaching these principles to the adult learners who attend the Osher courses at the University of Missouri, St. Charles Community College, and St. Louis Community College. Over the years much of this material has been derived from the courses that he has taught and feedback received from his students.

If you have a hunger for learning and a burning desire to create, keep, and maintain wealth for you and your family, we hope that you will enjoy this book.

OUR CLIENTS CAN EXPECT FROM US
Excellence
Empowerment
Relentless Execution

SECTION I

HOW DID WE GET HERE?

CHAPTER 1

THE LION AND THE GAZELLE

Which are you?

"Every morning in Africa, a gazelle awakens. It knows it must run faster than the fastest lion or it will be eaten. Every morning a lion wakes up. It knows it must outrun the slowest gazelle or it will starve to death. It doesn't matter whether you are a lion or a gazelle...when the sun comes up, you'd better be running!"

This parable hung on my mother's sewing room wall for years. Today, it keeps me company in my office and reminds me of the lessons she taught me. A lion knows exactly what it must do each day to feed itself and survive. It has clarity of goals (eating or starving), a plan (stalk gazelles), urgency (I'm hungry now and will be hungrier later), and purpose (to capture its prey). And, he monitors progress—is the belly full?

While a gazelle knows it must run to save its life and for survival, it is always playing defense. A gazelle reminds me of someone who just runs around like a crazy person with no sense of purpose or a plan, just running and trying to survive, day to day. All it knows is that the lion is after him and that it must run. The gazelle must outrun or outsmart the lion in order to survive. What if it begins running, but happens to run the wrong way? No second chances. A lion can go a day without eating, but the gazelle gets no second chance. For him, it's running with no sense of purpose or plan. Just run to survive.

A Broken System

The analogy of the lion and the gazelle emulates the present-day world of retirement planning. To put it simply, the system is broken.

According to the EBRI Retirement Security Projection Model, which was developed in 2003 and has been updated numerous times since, an estimated 40.6% of all U.S. households headed by someone aged 35 to 64 are projected to run short of money during retirement. This is based on a database of 27 million 401(k) participants and IRA account holders. This seems like a whole lot of households that are going to run short.

We are all living longer. In fact, longevity may be one of the most dangerous factors in outliving our retirement savings.

For those couples who reach age 65, 50% will have one partner live past 92, and 25% will have one partner live past 96. That means either you or your spouse has a one-in-four chance of having to make it through 31 years of retirement.

Of the top 10 greatest fears for most people, number five is "not having enough money for the future." The good news is that if you have done some planning, been a pretty good steward of your money, it doesn't have to be this way!

LionsGate Advisors, headquartered in Chesterfield, Missouri, is a true wealth strategy practice. We are fiduciaries. That should not be a unique fact or a selling point. It is *the* most rudimentary requirement. It should be assumed, not a sales story.

Fiduciary advice should be given by a team of strategists that is truly independent.
All recommendations must be in the best interest of the client. You should expect nothing less.

LionsGate Advisors is the only fee-based wealth management firm in the St. Louis area that quarterbacks key strategies for converting tax liabilities to assets. Our clients are affluent individuals, business owners, and family offices who want to build prosperity for a greater purpose. Our sole purpose is to accelerate the impact of our clients' wealth. It's not only what we do, it's what our clients expect.

Our Difference: How we make a difference for our clients.

Accelerating the impact of wealth requires one to successfully overcome three challenges. We call these the 3 P's:

- Purpose – clear and collectively understood goals
- Plan – well-thought-out plan aligned towards achievement of those goals
- Progress – a system to measure and adjust the path towards those goals

Our philosophy is clear. Each family or business we represent is different, as different as individual members of any family. **Anyone who is successful in their business or professional occupation has a process they follow based upon fact and logic.** An engineer would never just assume a beam span on a long bridge would be "about right," she would insist on a mathematical formula that takes into consideration the tensile strength of the steel, the length of the span, etc. A physician doesn't guess on which medication to use for a patient or which dose to prescribe, but uses a process to determine the diagnosis and then utilizes evidence-based medicine to determine a treatment. There is always a follow-up appointment to monitor the treatment and any changes in the patient's response to the treatment. A teacher doesn't show up for the year's classes with a rough idea of what to teach but has lesson plans and knows where she will go each week. She monitors the progress of the class by testing and scoring. She then adjusts her curriculum to address areas of misunderstanding.

In each of the above examples, the engineer, the physician, and the teacher utilize a formula based upon fact and logic. There are no shortcuts. Direction is based upon experience and facts. Assumption isn't a factor. Yet, in the world of financial planning we often throw out the methodical approach that made us successful, and instead accept decisions made on emotion and sales pressure. "He's got a great office; he's a friend of my brother; he took me to play golf. Must be a good planner."

Understanding and seeking clarity of purpose and goals is where it all begins.
Only then can a written plan be created.

A non-verified 1979 Harvard MBA study on goal setting analyzed the graduating class to determine how many had set goals and had a plan for their attainment. In the study, the graduating class was asked a single question about their goals in life. The question was this:

Have you set written goals and created a plan for their attainment?

Prior to graduation, it was determined that:
- 84% of the entire class had set no goals at all
- 13% of the class had set written goals but had no concrete plans
- 3% of the class had both written goals and concrete plans

The results?
You've probably guessed it. Ten years later, the 13% of the class who had set written goals but had not created plans were making twice as much money as the 84% of the class that had set no goals at all.

How about that other group? *The 3% who had both written goals and concrete plans? Ten years post-graduation, that group was making 10 times as much as the other 97% of the class.* As the fable from the chapter's beginning shows us, the individuals who planned and executed had more stability and control. Which of these groups of people would you describe as lions? Who are the gazelles? Which one would you most like to be?

Clearly, having clarity around **purpose and goals** as well as a **written plan** is essential. Also, having a reliable way to **monitor the progress** of the plan is what makes it all work. Many financial planners run the so-called Monte Carlo Simulation for Forecasting, a stress test and scenario analysis.

Stress testing is a computer-simulated technique to analyze how banks and investment portfolios fare in drastic economic scenarios. Stress testing helps to gauge investment risk and the adequacy of assets, as well as to help evaluate internal processes and controls. This type of stress testing can be used for modeling probabilities of various outcomes given specific variables. Factors considered in the Monte Carlo Simulation, for example, often include various economic variables.

A thousand sequences of return are analyzed and the probability of your plan being successful for your life expectancy is then displayed as a percentage of success. For an example of a thousand simulations, one would want to be in the 85-100% range, meaning of a thousand 'tests' you would be successful 85-1,000 times (lifetimes).

This is a powerful stress test for a plan, but our experience shows that the only lifetime our client is interested in is the one they are living!

The third part of a successful retirement plan is having a way to monitor the progress of the plan. In his song "Beautiful Boy" from the *Double Fantasy* album, John Lennon sang, "Before you cross the street take my hand. Life is what happens to you while you're busy making other plans."

We know that "things" change for families, the economy, the markets and the world in general.

My wife, Kimetha, and I are lifelong blue ocean sailors. Between the two of us, we have three transatlantic crossings, an Italy-to-

Singapore voyage, and countless other cruises in small (relatively) sailboats. In my office is a framed chart of the North Atlantic Ocean that we used on a voyage from Gibraltar to St. Martin in the Caribbean via the Canary Islands. We made the trip on a 48-foot sailboat with a crew of six. The return trip east took us from the British Virgin Islands (Caribbean) to Gibraltar via the Azores Islands. In total, we were at sea for more than a month.

Before we left Gibraltar to sail west, our yacht underwent "shakedown" cruises, intent on finding anything that might break prior to the voyage. We studied weather patterns to determine the best time of the year to cross. November proved most prudent for our east to west trip since it fell between the end of the hurricane season and the beginning of the northers.

We studied pilot books and charts with the aim of finding the best route, taking into consideration currents, wind direction and waves. The boat was stocked with food for a 30-day voyage (even though the actual planned voyage was closer to 15 days). Tools and spare parts were inventoried to ensure they would be available if and when needed. Our navigation instruments included everything from satellite GPS receivers to a sextant. Charts and both manual and automatic plotters were aboard. If the electronics failed, the manual methods would be utilized. Emergency supplies including life raft, EPRIB (Emergency Locator Beacon), radios and more were placed aboard and ready to use. Every possibility was taken into consideration and the crew was experienced.

Yet, when she set off, there was no guarantee the weather and the seas and the boat would run as planned. She had to be ready for any possibility. Once at sea, the position of the boat needed for a successful landfall in St. Martin was checked several times a day, plotted on the chart, and adjustments made as currents, wind, and weather demanded.

The successful crossing was made. I attribute the success to preparing and having clarity on the goals (landing intact on the *right* island), having a plan in place, and then careful monitoring of the progress of that plan.

The journey was successful because every possibility was planned for. As factors that affected the strategy came up, changes were made.

For our clients, it is much the same in their retirement plans.

As previously written in my book, *Accelerated Wealth, Real Planning for Today's Economy*, copyright 2016:

The Greek language is rich with meaning far beyond the English language. For instance, the word "time" has two different meanings in Greek. The word *kairos* is an ancient Greek word meaning opportunity, season, or fitting time. Another Greek word for time is *chronos*. A sequence of moments was expressed as *chronos*, emphasizing the duration of the time; an appointed time was expressed as *kairos*, with no regard for the length of the time. Thus, *chronos* was more linear and quantitative, and *kairos* was more nonlinear and qualitative.

Chronos is man's time. When the physician tells a young couple that their new baby will be born on January 31st that is chronos or man's time. When the father rushes the new mom to the hospital on the 28th that is kairos, or God's time. He didn't respond to his wife's insistence that it was time, saying, "No honey, the doctor said the baby is coming on the 31st." He rushed to the hospital and the baby was born soon after.

This is truly the story of God's time, kairos. With so many retiring and looking to retirement, it is the season, it is the fitting time, it is the time for the opportunity, to find a better way to plan and retire.

LionsGate Advisors was founded on the premise that we cannot be all things to all people, but rather all things to a select few. We are on a mission to help people truly understand their finances with no mumbo-jumbo or computer programs spitting out a plan. For you, this book is written with love, another word that has meanings in Greek that are so much more vibrant than they are in English. I share with you the LionsGate Advisors retirement strategies with Agape love—love expecting nothing in return but that you find peace and security in your work and retirement.

The Lion's Roar:
<u>Key Takeaways from Chapter 1</u>
- Be a lion, not a gazelle.
- Evaluate your financial advisor carefully (who is their #1 priority?).
- Take control of your choices. Be the Lion and remember, knowledge applied is power!

CHAPTER 2

NOW WHAT?

You are 10 days into retirement.

Your friends and family threw you a great retirement party.

You don't *have* to get up early anymore. In fact, you tried to sleep in late for the first couple of days. You tried staying up later at night. You enjoyed a few drinks after dinner. You started a couple of books you had been meaning to read for a long time. None of it helped.

Sunrise is only an hour away and your mind is racing. Counting sheep hasn't helped one iota. In fact, the sheep have a way of becoming dollar signs while your mind keeps going back to the spreadsheet you created with such care in anticipation of retirement.

You keep visualizing the meeting you had six weeks ago with your current financial planner. You can see your last statement from TD like it was opened in front of you right now. You just had a physical, and the doc says you could easily live another 25-30 years. That's good news, right?

You always managed your own 401(k), because you consider yourself pretty good with numbers. Sure, the account had some tough years, but it always came back.

But now you have more time on your hands. You spend a bit more time researching the stocks, listening to the talking heads' message on the television today, the latest news from the Federal Reserve, the national debt, taxes. What if you missed something? What if inflation doubled? What if there really was a sovereign debt crisis? What about Extended Care? What if you die before your spouse? Congress and the president can't ever seem to work together. How do you take control?

Now, exhausted, you fall asleep but when you awaken the endless chatter picks up from where you were before: what if, what if, what if???

Your whole life has been about planning and then executing the plan. You had years of experience and in your work, you learned from a mistake here or there, but this is your life, you have only one life to live and you don't have the luxury of training wheels or a second chance. The 40 years you worked and all you saved must last your lifetime. There are no do-overs.

All you want is for that endless chatter in your mind to stop as you lie awake. You need a sounding board, a trusted guide, a quarterback. And, most importantly, a team to ask the right questions to cut through the nonstop static in your head, to help you create a concise and realistic action plan.

The Lion's Roar:
Key Takeaways from Chapter 2

- Plan for more retirement years than you think you'll need. Don't plan to die, plan to live.
- Get expert assistance in managing your assets. Make sure you are working with a fiduciary. It is what you should expect.

CHAPTER 3

2020 - 2029 & BEYOND ECONOMIC FORECAST

Our national election process devotes quite a lot of ink and airtime to tax plan talk. One party says they will save you money! The other claims to be staving off certain economic catastrophe! Bet you can't tell which party is which. That's because neither of our two main political parties runs our government the way the rest of us are required to regulate our business and household finances. Though both would like to stake the moral high ground, the truth of our country's fiscal situation is revealed when you just look at the numbers.

Regardless of your political beliefs, much of this book is about math. Right, left, center, all the principles of math are the same. Tax cuts, entitlement programs, GDP (Gross Domestic Product) all just add up to simple math.

None of us could possibly run our individual finances or our businesses the way our favorite uncle, Uncle Sam, does.
The math just won't work.

Three types of economic indicators exist in the economy: leading, lagging, and coincident. Leading indicators attempt to predict future events; for instance, speculating bond yields or commodity futures are common leading indicators. Lagging indicators represent information that has already happened. Unemployment rates are a common lagging indicator. Coincident economic indicators usually are calculated at the same time the economic event occurs. The personal income indicator is a classic example of coincident indicators (Osmond Vitez, "How Are Economic Indicators Used by Analysts?").

Automobile production is seen as an accurate leading indicator. According to this year's AOS (the 2019 Automotive Outlook Symposium) consensus forecast, the economy is expected to grow at a solid but moderating pace in 2019 and 2020. The growth rate of real GDP is predicted to be 2.3% in 2019 and 1.9% in 2020. The unemployment rate is anticipated to remain below 4% through the end of 2020 *(Chicago Fed Letter, No. 417, 2019* "Economic Growth to Decelerate in 2019 and Then Ease Further in 2020 as Auto Sales Downshift," William A. Strauss , Kelley Sarussi).

The newest budget was passed and, once again, the U.S. government spends more than it collects in revenue. The deficit for 2020 is over $1 trillion and counting.

The CBO (Congressional Budget Office) projects deficits and debt regularly. In CBO's projections, federal budget deficits remain large by historical standards. Federal debt grows to equal 95% of GDP by 2029. Economic growth is expected to slow from 2.3% in 2019 to a rate that is below its long-run historical average.

CBO regularly publishes reports that present projections of what federal deficits, debt, revenues, and spending—and the economic path underlying them—would be for the current year and for the next 10 years if existing laws governing taxes and spending generally remained unchanged. This report is the latest in that series.

Deficits

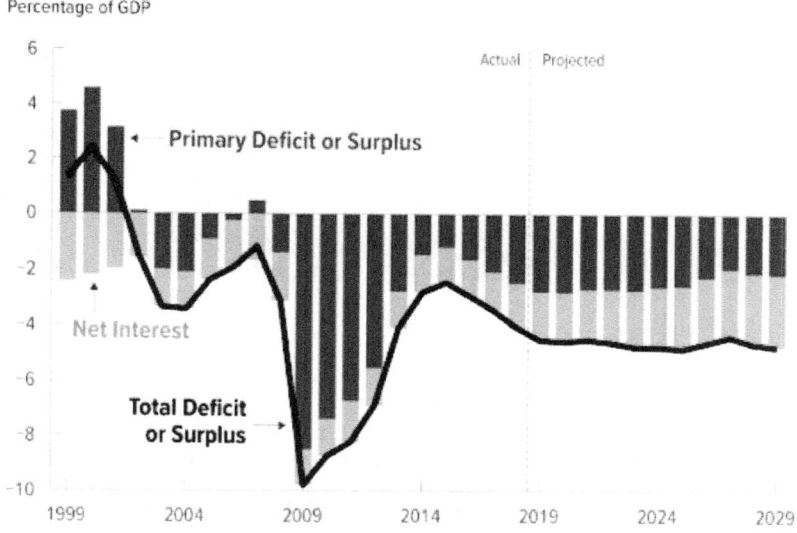

In CBO's projections, the federal budget deficit is $960 billion in 2019 and averages $1.2 trillion between 2020 and 2029. Over the coming decade, deficits (after adjustments to exclude the effects of shifts in the timing of certain payments) fluctuate between 4.4% and 4.8% of gross domestic product (GDP), well above the average over the past 50 years. Although both revenues and outlays grow faster than GDP over the next 10 years in CBO's baseline projections, the gap between the two persists.

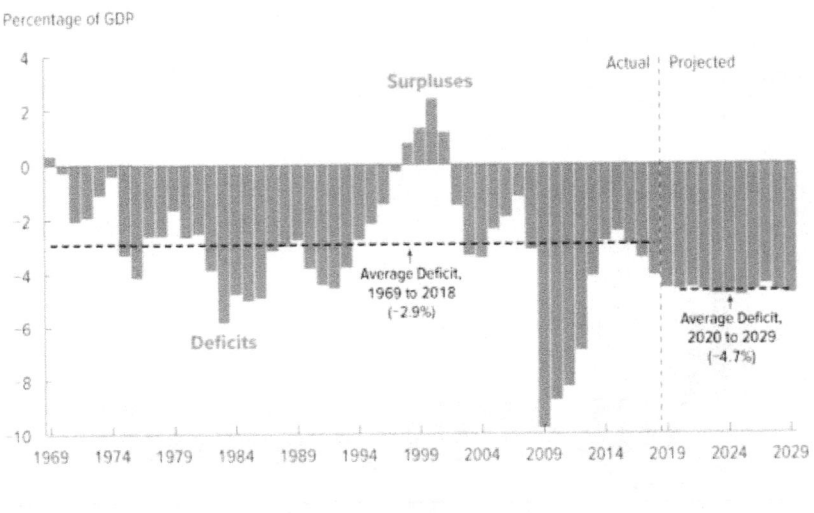

Does it seem like the U.S. Government plays by a different set of accounting rules? There is a reason for this—they do. Congress has the ability to legitimize its accounting systems and practices through legislation. If any of us tried to run our individual finances or business using the accounting system the government uses, we would be in prison for financial fraud and tax evasion. Congress and the U.S. Government are above the laws which they have mandated for the rest of us. For an individual or business, if you max out your existing lines of credit, you have to convince your banker you are credit worthy to gain additional financing. Congress just has to pass legislation to increase the debt ceiling. If the rest of us were allowed to operate this way, chaos would rule (*Accelerated Wealth, Real Financial Planning for Today's Economy*, Jason Ingram 2016)!

The Lost Decade

Largest daily point gains[6]

Rank	Date	Close	Change Net	Change %	Ref
1	2020-03-24	20,704.91	+2,112.98	+11.37	[7]
2	2020-03-13	23,185.62	+1,985.00	+9.36	[8]
3	2020-04-06	22,679.99	+1,627.46	+7.73	[9]
4	2020-03-26	22,552.17	+1,351.62	+6.38	[10]
5	2020-03-02	26,703.32	+1,293.96	+5.09	[11]
6	2020-03-04	27,090.86	+1,173.45	+4.53	[12]
7	2020-03-10	25,018.16	+1,167.14	+4.89	[13]
8	2018-12-26	22,878.45	+1,086.25	+4.98	[14]
9	2020-03-17	21,237.38	+1,048.86	+5.20	[15]
10	2008-10-13	9,387.61	+936.42	+11.08	[16]
11	2008-10-28	9,065.12	+889.35	+10.88	[17]
12	2020-04-08	23,433.57	+779.71	+3.44	[18]
13	2019-01-04	23,433.16	+746.94	+3.29	[19]
14	2020-04-17	24,242.49	+704.81	+2.99	[20]
15	2020-03-30	22,327.48	+690.70	+3.19	[21]
16	2018-03-26	24,202.60	+669.40	+2.84	[22]
17	2015-08-26	16,285.51	+619.07	+3.95	[23]
18	2018-11-28	25,366.42	+617.70	+2.50	[24]
19	2018-02-06	24,912.77	+567.02	+2.33	[25]
20	2020-04-14	23,949.76	+560.25	+6.67	[26]

Largest daily point losses[6]

Rank	Date	Close	Change Net	Change %	Ref
1	2020-03-16	20,188.52	-2,997.10	-12.93	[27]
2	2020-03-12	21,200.62	-2,352.60	-9.99	[28]
3	2020-03-09	23,851.02	-2,013.76	-7.79	[29]
4	2020-03-11	23,553.22	-1,464.94	-5.86	[30]
5	2020-03-18	19,898.92	-1,338.46	-6.30	[31]
6	2020-02-27	25,766.64	-1,190.95	-4.42	[32]
7	2018-02-05	24,344.72	-1,172.29	-4.60	[33]
8	2018-02-08	23,860.46	-1,032.89	-4.15	[34]
9	2020-02-24	27,960.80	-1,031.61	-3.56	[35]
10	2020-04-01	20,943.51	-973.65	-4.44	[36]
11	2020-03-05	26,121.28	-969.58	-3.58	[37]
12	2020-03-27	21,636.78	-915.42	-4.06	[38]
13	2020-03-20	19,173.98	-913.21	-4.55	[39]
14	2020-02-25	27,081.36	-879.44	-3.15	[40]
15	2018-10-10	25,598.74	-831.83	-3.15	[41]
16	2019-08-14	25,479.42	-800.49	-3.05	[42]
17	2018-12-04	25,027.07	-799.36	-3.10	[43]
18	2020-03-03	25,917.41	-785.91	-2.94	[44]
19	2008-09-29	10,365.45	-777.68	-6.98	[45]
20	2019-08-05	25,717.74	-767.27	-2.90	[46]

Source: Wikipedia

I can still see it as if it were yesterday. I was in a small meeting at the Tampa, Florida home of Peter G, the VP of Development at the large venture capital group where I worked in Mergers & Acquisition (M&A). Ten of us regional sales managers were seated in

Peter's family room, sipping on mineral water, all facing the TV. Were we watching the baseball playoffs? No. The meeting agenda was, initially, to discuss upcoming strategies for 2009, but the day's news had driven a bulldozer through any possible planning we could do. We all were glued to the TV, mouths agape, as we watched the stock tickers fall…and fall…and fall.

The stock market crash of 2008-09 began on October 11, 2007 and lasted until closing low on March 9, 2009 (a retracement of 61.8%). On October 15, 2007, the Dow Jones Industrial Average fell 777.68 points in intra-day trading. Until 2020 and the COVID-19 recession (the Dow dropped 2,997.10 on March 16), it was the largest point drop in history. It plummeted because Congress rejected the bank bailout. But the stresses that led to the crash had been building for a long time.

On October 9, 2007, the Dow hit its pre-recession high and closed at 14,164.53. By March 5, 2009, it had dropped more than 50% to 6,594.44.

Although it wasn't the greatest percentage decline in history, it was vicious (the Great Depression decline was 90%, but that stretched out over a four-year period). The markets continued with much volatility, finally bottoming out in March. On March 5, 2009, the Dow plummeted to its bottom of 6,594.44 (from a high of 13,264.82).

We call this period of time The Lost Decade. In the U.S., the period between 2000 and 2009 witnessed a massive erosion of wealth. The economy had the slowest period of economic growth in the U.S. in decades. The S&P 500 recorded its all-time worst decade during this period, featuring a total return of dividends at

-9.1%, an overall performance lower than during the Great Depression of the 1930s.

Basically, if you put a dollar in the market in 2000, by the end of 2009, it was worth about a dollar.

Part of this volatility was caused by flash trading. The term flash trading refers to the practice of using high-speed computers and low-latency communication lines to view orders before they reach the general marketplace. As is the case with high-frequency trading, flash trading is limited to those institutions with direct feeds to an exchange.

The ability to engage in flash trading is limited to large institutional investors, hedge funds, and investment banks. These traders use sophisticated computer hardware and software algorithms to deliver a large number of orders at a very high speed to an exchange. The ability to analyze market conditions and execute orders at these speeds provides the users of these systems with a trading advantage in the marketplace.

Also known as flash orders, flash trading involves submitting and cancelling a large number of small orders to find larger orders that the trader is able to buy or sell before the order even reaches the market. This practice can occur in dark pools, where there is less transparency with respect to the bid and ask prices of securities. High-speed computers are not only used to flood the market with orders, but also to predict potential price trends.

This is because flash trading has an edge. Its sophisticated computing power allows traders to view orders from other market participants fractions of a second before others in the marketplace. This gives flash traders the advantage of being able to gauge supply and demand and recognize movements in market sentiment before other traders.

America suffered another mini-economic crisis on May 6, 2010. This has become known as the May 6, 2010 Flash Crash, aka The Crash of 2:45. During this Flash Crash, the Dow Jones Industrial Average plunged about 1,000 points (about 9%) only to recover those losses within minutes. It was the second largest point swing, 1,010.14 points, and the biggest one-day point decline, 998.5 points, on an intra-day basis in Dow Jones Industrial Average history.

The Lion's Roar:
Key Takeaways from Chapter 3
- The government is playing by a different financial rulebook than the rest of us.
- Retirement accounts lost enormous ground in growth between 2000 and 2009.
- Volatility in the markets can dramatically change your retirement. Utilize non-correlated assets for a true diversification.

CHAPTER 4

IT'S JUST MATH

What's a four-letter word that is not emotional nor changes with time? Math. Math is the word to which we should all be paying attention.

At the time of publication in 2020, we are on the precipice of an economic storm that has the potential to change our lives, our retirement, and our children's lives in dramatic fashion.

The last time the country had a budget surplus was in 2001, the first full year of the George W. Bush presidency. Bill Clinton had maintained a surplus from 1998-2000.

31 Flavors of Debt
The deficit in 2000 began a dangerous pattern of overspending that culminated with the recession of 2008 and the highest deficit ever recorded in 2009 of $1.4 trillion with the bank crisis and bailout, the Stimulus Act, and the Obama tax cuts. In 2011 and 2012, the deficit topped $1.1 trillion. In 2013, the deficit halved to $680 billion, went down again in 2014 to $485 billion. After that, it slowly climbed back up to $585 billion in the election year of 2016.

The election of Donald Trump brought a new fiscal reality to America and the world. Concrete Republican values like elimination of budget deficits, balanced spending, free trade went out the window as he ushered in a new kind of governing and accountability. His advisors, hand selected, along with control of both houses of Congress, began new economic policies that promoted tax cuts, tariffs, and a semi-isolationist vision of the world—America First. Whereas past Republican administrations, and Republican-controlled Congress, worked to balance budgets and cut spending, the new sheriff promoted and passed the Tax Cuts and Jobs Act (TCJA) of 2017, reducing taxes both corporately and individually. The individual and pass-through tax cuts fade over time and become net tax increases starting in 2027 while the corporate tax cuts are permanent.

These cuts were touted as a solution that would increase revenue and expand business. To date (February 2020), this has not happened as was promised. At the same time, the deficit has risen to extremely high levels in spite of a pretty robust economy.

Quarterly GDP at market prices 2019			
Date	Quarterly GDP	Quat. GDP Growth (%)	Quat. GDP Annual Growth (%)
2019Q3	5,385,635M.$	0.5%	2.1%
2019Q2	5,335,067M.$	0.5%	2.0%
2019Q1	5,274,707M.$	0.8%	3.1%
< GDP United States 2018			

The predictions of a GDP of 4 to 5% have not proven to be warranted. Growth has hovered at around 2 to 3%. Cue the sad trombone. In a report released in March 2019, the president's economic team predicted that growth would slow to about 2% a year in 2026. That is the year when many of the individual tax cuts included in the 2017 law are set to expire, essentially producing a tax increase for millions of Americans.

The national debt—aka the federal debt—is the total of all the past years' budget deficits, minus what the government has paid off with budget surpluses. Currently this figure stands at $23 trillion dollars and is rising every second (see National Debt Clock at http://www.usdebtclock.org.).

Even more disturbing are the unfunded liabilities. (Unfunded liabilities are debt obligations that do not have sufficient funds set aside to pay the debt.) These liabilities generally refer to debts of the U.S. Government or of pension plans and their impact on savings and investment securities. Unfunded liabilities can have significant and negative impact on the general economic health of a nation or corporation.

Unfunded liabilities are estimated as of early 2020 to be $127.5 trillion and rising.

In finance and economics, a liability is a legal obligation of a person, organization or government entity to pay a debt arising from a past or current transaction or action. In brief, a liability is a claim on the debtor's current or future assets. An unfunded liability is a liability that does not have current or projected assets to cover the liability; therefore, it is said to be unfunded.

In reference to the U.S. Government, a prime example of an unfunded liability is Social Security. When Social Security was first implemented by Franklin D. Roosevelt in 1935, there were more than enough payees (working taxpayers) to support the number of Social Security beneficiaries (retirees). In 1940, the ratio of payees to beneficiaries was 159 to one. Today the ratio of workers to beneficiaries is less than three to one. Medicare has a similar problem with unfunded liabilities *(The Washington Free Beacon*, "Unfunded Liabilities of State Public Pensions Top $6 Trillion in 2017," Retrieved November 11, 2019).

The personal debt load of Americans is a factor. **On average, each household with a credit card carries $8,398 in credit card debt.** Total U.S. consumer debt is at $13.86 trillion. That includes mortgages, auto loans, credit cards and student loans ("Key Figures Behind America's Consumer Debt" Debt.org https://www.debt.org › faqs › americans-in-debt).

Student loan debt is growing quickly and also threatens stability of the system. Paying for college has turned into a long-term burden for millions of Americans. As I write these words in early January 2020, the total bill is $1.6 trillion, or $36,670 per student, which is more than double what it was a decade earlier. About 66% of students who earned four-year degrees in 2017 took out loans and owed $28,500 when they got their caps and gowns. Of the 42.2 million people with federal student loans, 2.7 million owed *at least $100,000*. The Fed's Survey of Consumer Finances shows that 22.4% of families had student loan debt in 2016.

Compare that crushing debt load to the previous generation. Only 8.9% of grads were paying such loans in 1989. The average family owed $5,400 in 1989. By the time pop radio switched from playing Bon Jovi to Justin Bieber, the money owed by the average graduate ballooned to $34,200. Even adjusted for inflation, that's a threefold increase. The average monthly payment was $339 a month (Bill Fey, staff writer for debt.org).

And then, there is the cost of health care. As fees continue to rocket out of control, health care as a whole now comprises about 18% of the U.S. GDP. Although it has steadied in recent years, inflation for health care runs at about 6.5% and the cost to GDP is staggering. Modernhealthcare.com estimates the cost of health care to GDP to increase to 19.7%.

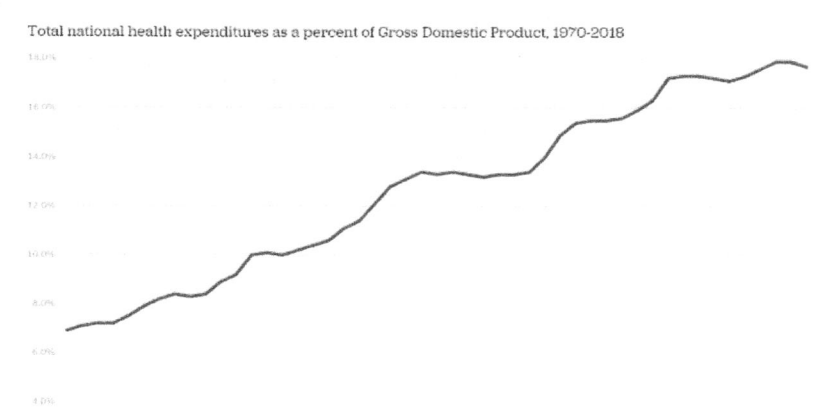

Health spending growth has outpaced growth of the U.S. economy

Total national health expenditures as a percent of Gross Domestic Product, 1970-2018

Inflation also adds velocity to the coming storm. Consider the following:

The last car you ever buy will cost more than your first house did.

The typical retired person or person nearing retirement will usually say they spent between $10,000 and $12,000 to purchase their first home. I then ask them to think about how much they paid for their last car. Ouch! That's a good example of inflation.

The Lion's Roar:
Key Takeaways from Chapter 4
- U.S. debt and deficits are going to come home to roost… probably sooner rather than later.
- Cost of living, especially health care and higher education, has far outpaced wage growth.
- Don't be caught flat-footed when taxes go up. Have a plan for tax-free income now!

CHAPTER 5

AGING POPULATION
A DEMOGRAPHIC TIME-BOMB

This demographic transformation caused by a rapidly aging population is new for the United States but not for other countries. Japan has the world's oldest population, where more than one in four people are at least 65 years old. Already, the country's population has started to decline; by 2050, it is projected to shrink by 20 million people. Since 2011, there are more adult diapers sold in Japan than infant diapers.

Europe is headed down the same demographic path. Some countries in Western Europe have populations that are older than the U.S., notably Germany, Italy, France, and Spain. Countries in Eastern Europe are even further along and, within a few years, many of their populations are projected to begin shrinking.

America has been different, until now.

With this swelling number of older adults, the country could see greater demands for health care, in-home caregiving and assisted living facilities. It could also affect Social Security. Demographers project that there will be three-and-a-half working-age adults for every older person eligible for Social Security in 2020.

By 2060, that number is expected to fall to two-and-a-half working-age adults for every older person.

If the trends continue, the U.S. is fast heading towards a demographic first. It will become grayer than ever before as older adults outnumber kids (US Census Bureau, "The Graying of America").

Taxes, Taxes, Taxes...
It may be apocryphal, but the story goes that bank robber, Willie Sutton, was asked, "Why do you rob banks?" To which he replied, "That's where the money is!" Your rich Uncle Sam looks at it the same way. Where and whom do we tax? Those who have money to pay. And—let me give you a hint—it's not Google, or Amazon, or General Electric. It's *YOU*. (*1951 January 20, The Saturday Evening Post, Volume 223, Issue 30,* "Someday They'll Get Slick Willie Sutton" by Robert M. Yoder, Start Page 17, Quote Page 17, Saturday Evening Post Society, Indianapolis, Indiana Academic Search Premier).

An in-depth analysis of Fortune 500 companies' financial filings finds that at least 60 of the nation's biggest corporations didn't pay a dime in federal income taxes in 2018 on a collective $79 billion in profits, according to the Institute on Taxation and Economic Policy (ITEP). Let me repeat that.

In 2018, the top 60 corporations in the country paid exactly zero dollars in taxes.

If these companies paid the statutory 21% federal tax rate, they would owe $16.4 billion in federal income taxes. Instead, they collectively received $4.3 billion in rebates. The analysis, *"Corporate Tax Avoidance Remains Rampant under New Tax Law,"* examines 2018 corporate financial filings that have been released to date. It provides an initial, comprehensive look at how corporate tax cuts under the 2017 Tax Cuts and Jobs Act affected the tax-paying habits of corporations.

The tax-avoiding corporations are some of the most profitable, recognizable companies in the world, and they represent a variety of industries, including technology, energy and gas, financial services, aviation, pharmaceutical and manufacturing. Earlier this year, ITEP reported Netflix and Amazon paid no federal taxes. Other companies on this list include Chevron, Delta Airlines, Eli Lilly, General Motors, Gannett, Goodyear Tire and Rubber, Halliburton, IBM, Jet Blue Airways, Principal Financial, Salesforce.com, US Steel, and Whirlpool. The complete list is at *https://itep.org/notadime. Courtesy of ITEP – Institute on Taxation & Economic Policy 2019.*

Now let's take a look at individual taxpayers. The chart below helps to illustrate the discrepancy in how much taxpayers are spending depending on income bracket.

Those of us who have been careful stewards, who have done *everything* right, saved money, utilized our 401(k) carefully, and saved and spent carefully to make sure we could retire comfortably are the ones in those last three columns. Together we make up 69% of those who pay taxes. The Pew Research Center indicates that taxpayers with adjusted gross incomes (AGI) in excess of $200,000 paid more than half of all taxes collected in 2015—58.9%, to be exact.

The chart below helps to illustrate the discrepancy in how much tax-payers are spending depending on income bracket.

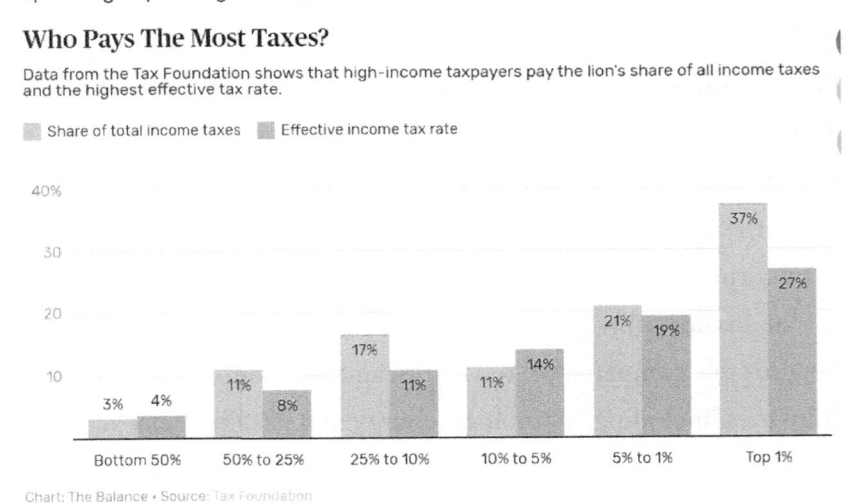

Who Pays The Most Taxes?

Data from the Tax Foundation shows that high-income taxpayers pay the lion's share of all income taxes and the highest effective tax rate.

■ Share of total income taxes   ■ Effective income tax rate

Bracket	Share of total income taxes	Effective income tax rate
Bottom 50%	3%	4%
50% to 25%	11%	8%
25% to 10%	17%	11%
10% to 5%	11%	14%
5% to 1%	21%	19%
Top 1%	37%	27%

Chart: The Balance • Source: Tax Foundation

About This Economic Train Wreck...

Have you ever watched the Wile E. Coyote cartoons where he is trying to outsmart the Road Runner? You may remember the episode where Wile E. has purchased an Acme shed and he is inside cutting the tops off of carrots (Acme carrots, of course) and filling them with explosives, all the while telling himself what a genius he is. In the meantime, unbeknownst to Wile E., the Road Runner has lassoed the shed and pulled it onto a railroad track. Wile E. goes about his work until he hears a train whistle. He stops, turns around and looks out the window and sees that a train is bearing down on the shed. Does he get off the track? No, he employs cartoon logic and pulls down the curtain. The train hits the shed, resulting in a giant *ka-blamo* explosion, blowing everything up including Wile E. Also following cartoon logic,

Wile E. is no worse for the experience except for some burned fur.

Not to overstate things, but we are in the same Acme shed.

Sovereign Debt Crisis
A sovereign debt crisis is when a country is unable to pay its bills. This doesn't happen overnight, as there are plenty of warning signs. It becomes a crisis when the country's leaders ignore these indicators for political reasons. The U.S. debt is the total financial obligation owed by the federal government. It is composed of, Public debt, reflected by Treasuries, and intragovernmental debt, what Treasury owes various gov- ernment departments, the largest portion being that owed to Social Security.

The United States holds the record for owning the largest sovereign debt by a single country in the world. Because of its high debt-to-GDP ratio, many worry about America's future ability to pay.

Five factors have caused U.S. debt to burgeon enormously:
- Accumulation of budget deficits
- Loans from the Social Security Trust Fund to fuel government spending
- Issuance of Treasuries to countries, such as China and Japan, which want to keep the value of their exports low
- Low interest rates which contributed to budget deficits
- Continuous raising of the debt ceiling by Congress

Many believe that U.S. debt is growing at an unsustainable rate. At a certain point, the current rate of creditor confidence could plummet along with the rising U.S. debt-to-GDP ratio. The resulting sovereign debt crisis may shackle many Americans to a poorer quality of life in the years to come, or taxes will have to increase.

Taxes are currently at all-time lows. A look at the tax rates on the highest AGI since the inception of the IRS in 1913 shows we are indeed in a very low tax time (*Urban.org*).

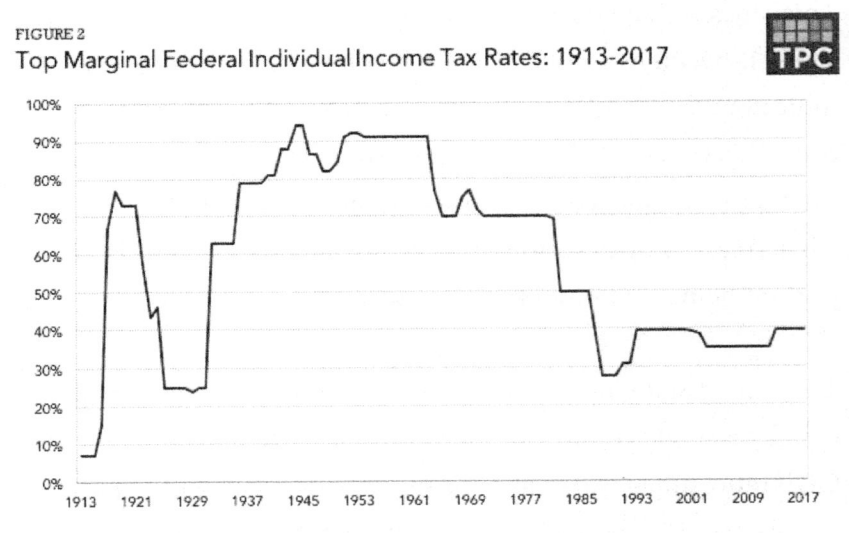

FIGURE 2
Top Marginal Federal Individual Income Tax Rates: 1913-2017

Source: "Historical Individual Income Tax Parameters," Tax Policy Center, May 5, 2017.

So, where does the revenue come from to meet all the unfunded liabilities and the current budget deficit? Remember the Willie Sutton story? It's where the money is! YOU!

When there isn't a single dollar left to be squeezed from entitlement programs, when the GDP can go no higher, your uncle will come calling, striped top-hat in hand.

At that point, it's not the 90% who pay the lowest taxes, it is those with $200k in income who pay 59.8% of all collected tax revenue. They already have your number and they are coming for more.

COVID-19 Update – November 2020
As I edit this manuscript, the global pandemic surrounding COVID-19 has hit full force in over 100 countries, including the United States where it is multiplying quickly. The U.S. now has the most cases of the virus and accounts for almost one-fifth of the worldwide deaths. South America, Latin America, and Africa are seeing outbreaks that will be difficult to control.

Congress and the Federal Reserve have acted to prop up financial markets, businesses, and to some extent the regular guy.

This global pandemic may have lasting effects on markets and certainly our public health. It is a seminal moment in time, much like the days after 9/11. We still don't really know the effect the virus will have going forward, as so many have had to restructure their lives and businesses around this new reality.

I believe it is safe to say, we will think of this as "Pre-COVID-19" and "Post- (hopefully) COVID-19." One thing is for sure, we will never look at the world again in quite the same way.

If you are reading this, you have survived the first wave. Our hope is that the second and third waves will not emulate the path the Spanish Flu took in 1918, which took about a quarter of the world's population (an estimated 20-40 million people).

However this new pandemic plays out, the economic measures Congress and POTUS have taken will add to the already worsening and potentially catastrophic path of debt this country is embarking upon. The phrase, "it's just math," doesn't quite represent the epic costs that we, as a country, are racking up—and the numbers will be staggering with the $2 trillion initial bailout for corporations, businesses, nonprofits and individuals.

Thus far, the U.S. Congress has given away two trillion dollars in COVID-19 bailout money. That's a 2 with 12 zeros after it. $2,000,000,000,000!

The Fed has lowered the interest rates to zero and has begun quantitative easing. *Quantitative easing (QE)* is a form of unconventional monetary policy in which a central bank purchases longer-term securities from the open market. Utilized during the Great Recession of 2008, QE is performed in order to increase the money supply and encourage lending and investment once again.

In an article from the *Washington Post*, March 28, 2020:

> In hindsight, however, the economy had blemishes. The record-high stock prices the president routinely touted became disconnected from companies' underlying value, obscuring warning signs such as excessive borrowing, according to economist Michalis Nikiforos of the Levy Economics Institute of Bard College. Total corporate debt surged past $10 trillion, equal to nearly one-half the nation's annual output.

"This shock does not come at a time when the economy is otherwise healthy," he said. "There are very significant fragilities in the U.S. economy and elsewhere."

On the eve of the crisis, one-quarter of the country's largest companies had more cash going out than coming in, according to Goldman Sachs. The economic shutdown will quickly cause the share of American companies that are cash-flow negative to nearly double, meaning they could be in danger of starving for funds.

David Lynch further analyzes the economy in this April 18, 2020 *Washington Post* article entitled, "Record Government and Corporate Debt Risks 'Tipping Point' After Pandemic Passes."

"The United States is embarking on a rapid-fire experiment in borrowing without precedent, as the government and corporations take on trillions of dollars of debt to offset the economic damage from the coronavirus pandemic.

The federal government is on its way this year to spending nearly $4 trillion more than it collects in revenue, analysts say, a budget deficit roughly twice as large relative to the economy as in any year since 1945."

Not to understate the case, but we are truly in uncharted territory. Businesses we are used to seeing in our everyday lives are failing and declaring bankruptcy. JC Penny, Dean & Deluca, Neiman Marcus, CMX Cinemas, J. Crew, Gold's Gym, Pier 1 Imports, Hertz, Tuesday Morning, GNC and Cirque du Soleil may cease to exist as we know them…or at all.

In order to support these businesses, the Federal Reserve has dropped interest rates to near zero. We have seen the PPP, Payroll Protection Plan, roll out and run out of money quickly.

Lynch's article continues:

"We should be very worried," said Atif Mian, an economics professor at Princeton University who has written widely on the subject. "We are talking about a level of debt that would certainly be unprecedented in modern history or in history, period. We are definitely at a tipping point."

I agree with the conclusions here. Massive borrowing has been utilized to prop up the economy with levels never seen before. In March, the Fed was purchasing over $75 billion of bonds daily. While it has cut back to around $30 billion a day, the amount of money being borrowed and pumped into the economy is worrisome. In 2010 during the recession, the Fed was purchasing $110 billion a month. In this crisis, the Fed is purchasing this much every four days!

This out-of-control spending will come home to roost and it won't be pretty.

If I were writing a 30-second TV spot attacking a free-spending Congress in 2020, I might have the voice actor deliver something like this. Read this in your soberest voice.

"This deal represents an unprecedented geyser of taxpayer money spurting forth with no offsetting revenues or spending cuts. Not only did Congress balloon the federal budget, they tripled this year's anticipated deficit of a trillion dollars (already at the highest in history). With this single vote, Congress has added as much to the national debt as was accumulated in the first two hundred years of the Constitution's existence."

Neither I nor anyone can predict what markets will do or react to monetary policy, but if we use simple math, we know there is a lot more being spent than is being replenished in the treasury. Ancient Rome had the same problem and it didn't turn out very well.

Time will tell, but by becoming educated to these new realities and taking steps today to ensure tax mitigation, no matter what the outcome—good or bad—you and your family will be well ahead of the game.

The families we serve at LionsGate Advisors are concerned and are taking measures now to make sure they are protected. To them, it's not a matter of *if* taxes go up, but *when*.

Shouldn't you be doing the same?

The Lion's Roar:
Key Takeaways from Chapter 5

- The U.S. population is aging. Corporations are paying next to nothing in taxes. All while America's debt-to-GDP ratio is the highest in the world. This cannot go on in perpetuity,

and the likeliest taxpayers to shoulder that burden are those who are reading this book.
- Wise readers are working toward shifting tax liabilities to assets which offer tax-advantaged growth and low risk.

CHAPTER 6

WHAT'S WRONG WITH THIS...

You are lying on a gurney in the cardiac intensive care unit at your local hospital. You're scared. You look at the ceiling and the lights and listen to the unfamiliar noises coming from the hallway. You're in a hospital gown; your head is hot, but your hands and feet are freezing. You're hooked up to multiple monitors that beep and flash. Nurses and physicians come and go quickly, moving from bed to bed. This is the ICU and you just had a heart attack.

While your terrified wife steps into the hall to call the kids, you take a moment to ponder your situation. The doctors are recommending a valve replacement to repair the damage. While they're in there, they'll RotoRooter your coronary arteries as well. These procedures have a high rate of success. You feel lucky that you didn't die. They say after the surgery you are going to feel so much better. Who knows how long those two arteries have been partially blocked and the valve malfunctioning? What if you had ignored that heaviness in your chest, rationalizing that it was probably heartburn?

Yeah, you're lucky to be alive. And you know it.

You're also lucky to live close to a large, university teaching hospital that has a renowned cardiac unit. They've seen it all.

They have the very latest technology and they do a lot of these procedures.

Earlier, when the cardiothoracic surgeon was talking to you and your wife, she explained how a valve replacement can now be done with minimally invasive surgery that minimizes incision size, recovery time, and infection risks by performing a trans-catheter aortic-valve replacement procedure, whereby a new heart valve will be placed via a catheter inserted through a small incision in the groin, then threaded through the vascular system and into the heart.

You are scared but you know you are in good hands. Your surgeon knows her stuff. She's the best.

But what if, what if...she had met with you and your wife to explain that the procedure they planned to use was one that hadn't advanced since the 1950s? What if instead of doing a replacement through your artery, she instead decided to perform open-heart surgery through a long incision down the center of the chest? Open-heart procedures do still occur in modern times but are far less frequent because of the higher risks and worse outcomes. What if, after explaining your options, your surgeon tells you that instead of using the most up-to-date surgical techniques and tools, they have opted to operate using tools from 1952?

Now, you are petrified.

I use this analogy because 95% of financial salespeople still use a system for diversification and allocation that was first introduced in 1952. Think about that for a minute.

The most commonly used tool to improve retirement yields hasn't advanced since 1952!

This tool has never seen an entire generation through retirement, and in the market corrections of 2000-2001 and 2007-08, it was an unmitigated disaster for many retirees and those close to retirement.

The system of allocation and diversification was introduced by Harry Markowitz in 1952. Thirty-eight years later he won the Nobel Prize in Economics for this work.

The Lion's Roar:
Key Takeaways from Chapter 6

- Most financial salespeople are using an antiquated, unproven tool to guide their clients.
- Would you have an operation today with surgical techniques and instruments from 1950?

CHAPTER 7

NO GOLD WATCHES

Beginning with the advent of the 401(k) in 1980, also known as *Defined Contribution Plans*, and then the use of Mutual Funds in these retirement plans, the door for the average investor was kicked wide open. No longer able to count on a *Defined Benefit Plan* (pension) from their employer, the onus for a successful retirement was moved from the company to the individual and the risks associated with it fell to the individual. Great for the companies, not so great for the employee. No more gold watches.

Reading between the lines, the message here is, "When it comes to retirement savings, don't count on your employer. You're on your own."

Ted Benna is widely regarded as the father of the 401(k), with the passage of the Revenue Act of 1978. The former benefits consultant didn't write the 869-word section of tax code that paved the way for the plan. Nor did he set out to reimagine how Americans saved for retirement. Yet, through what he calls a political "fluke" and his own interest in helping a client, Benna played a role in doing just that. In the decades since, assets in 401(k) plans have swelled to more than $5 trillion—and the impact is probably double that if you count rollovers to individual retirement accounts.

In order to better understand why we don't have the defined benefit plan or pension and now have a 401(k) or some derivative of that, we have to go back to Studebaker-Packard and, after their demise, the formation of ERISA by Congress in 1974.

Portfolio Theory: A Bit of History
Modern portfolio theory (MPT)—or portfolio theory—was introduced by Harry Markowitz with his paper "Portfolio Selection," which appeared in the 1952 *Journal of Finance*. Thirty-eight years later, he shared the Nobel Prize with Merton Miller and William Sharpe for what has become a broad theory for portfolio selection.

Prior to Markowitz's work, investors focused on assessing the risks and rewards of individual securities in constructing their portfolios. Standard investment advice was to identify those securities that offered the best opportunities for gain with the least risk and then construct a portfolio from these.

Following this advice, an investor might conclude that railroad stocks all offered good risk-reward characteristics and compile a portfolio entirely from these. Intuitively, this would be foolish. Markowitz formalized this intuition. Detailing a mathematics of diversification, he proposed that investors focus on selecting portfolios based on their overall risk-reward characteristics instead of merely compiling portfolios from securities that individually have attractive risk-reward characteristics.

In a nutshell, investors should select portfolios, not individual securities. (riskglossary.com)

What is Efficient Frontier?
Different combinations of securities produce different levels of return. The *efficient frontier* represents the best of these securities combinations: those that produce the maximum expected return for a given level of risk. The efficient frontier is the basis for modern portfolio theory.

How Does Efficient Frontier Work?
In 1952, Harry Markowitz published a formal portfolio selection model in *The Journal of Finance.* He continued to develop and publish research on the subject over the next 20 years, eventually winning the 1990 Nobel Prize in Economics for his work on the efficient frontier and other contributions to modern portfolio theory.

According to Markowitz, for every point on the efficient frontier, there is at least one portfolio that can be constructed from all available investments that has the expected risk and return corresponding to that point.

An example appears below. Note how the *efficient frontier* allows investors to understand how a portfolio's expected returns vary with the amount of risk taken.

The relationship securities have with each other is an important part of the *efficient frontier*. Some securities' prices move in the same direction under similar circumstances, while others move in opposite directions. The more out of sync the securities in the portfolio are (that is, the lower their covariance), the smaller the risk (standard deviation) of the portfolio that combines them. The *efficient frontier* is curved because there is a diminishing marginal return to risk. Each unit of risk added to a portfolio gains a smaller and smaller amount of return.

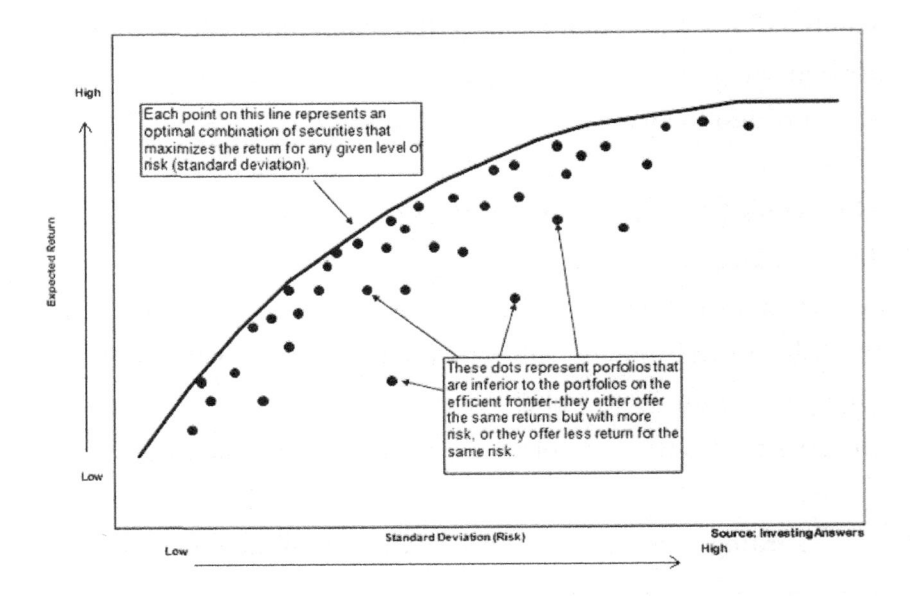

[Figure: Efficient frontier graph plotting Expected Return (Low to High) against Standard Deviation/Risk (Low to High). A curved line represents the efficient frontier with scattered dots below it. Annotations read: "Each point on this line represents an optimal combination of securities that maximizes the return for any given level of risk (standard deviation)." and "These dots represent portfolios that are inferior to the portfolios on the efficient frontier—they either offer the same returns but with more risk, or they offer less return for the same risk." Source: InvestingAnswers]

Why Does Efficient Frontier Matter?

When Markowitz introduced the *efficient frontier*, it was groundbreaking in many respects. One of its largest contributions was its clear demonstration of the power of diversification.

Markowitz's theory relies on the claim that investors tend to choose, either on purpose or inadvertently, portfolios that generate the largest possible returns with the least amount of risk. In other words, they seek out portfolios on the *efficient frontier*.

However, there is no one *efficient frontier*, because portfolio managers and investors can edit the number and characteristics of the securities in the investing universe to conform to their specific needs. For example, a client may require the portfolio to have a minimum dividend yield, or the client may rule out investments in ethically or politically undesirable industries. Only the remaining securities are included in the *efficient frontier* calculations *(Investing Answers, October 2019)*.

What is Standard Deviation?

Standard deviation is a measure of how much an investment's returns can vary from its average return. It is a measure of volatility and in turn, risk. The formula for standard deviation is:

Standard Deviation = $[1/n * (r_i - r_{ave})2]^{½}$

where:
r_i = actual rate of return
r_{ave} = average rate of return
n = number of time periods

(Investing Answers, October 2019)

Harry Markowitz is a well-respected and true pioneer in digging deep into the world of risk and correlation (or actually non-correlation) of portfolios. At age 92 (as of this writing in 2020), he continues to work as a professor of finance at the Rady School of Management at the University of California, San Diego.

Putting the Lessons to Work

Working with individuals over the years and on my own portfolios has helped me to see how important non-correlation is, and also to develop different models of this premise that combine less risk with true non-correlation.

If one were to go into an apple grove and begin picking five apples from every tree in the grove with the intent of having a basket of different types of apples, it would be important to know if the grove was all McIntosh apples.

Just because each tree yielded apples that you chose, if they are the same variety, you have a nice basket of the same apple type.

So it is with creating a truly non-correlated wealth strategy. In our practice, we have seen clients ages 35-95 come into our conference room, bringing with them all their statements.

Some have Fidelity accounts, some T. Rowe Price, some Schwab, some TD Ameritrade, some with their local bank's trust department. Others have all of the above and many more accounts they have opened over the years. Some are IRAs they have rolled over from 401(k) accounts. Some have non-qualified accounts (A *non-qualifying* investment is an investment that does not *qualify* for any level of tax-deferred or tax-exempt status. Investments of this sort are made with after-tax money. They are purchased and held in tax-deferred *accounts,* plans, or trusts. Returns from these investments are taxed on an annual basis).

After completing an analysis on these holdings, one thing almost always stands out: they've picked a lot of apples *and all are from the same grove.*

One other discovery trend I've noticed among clients who are in retirement or close to retirement is this. Most of them have what I call "portfolio disconnect." Portfolio disconnect is what can happen when you retire or get one to five years from retirement. While you are/were working, you saved as much as you could toward retirement. You were in an accumulation period of your life.

Money poured in; some you tried to save, some went into tax-deferred accounts like 401(k) or SEP or 457 or other qualified accounts. (Qualified plans have tax-deferred contributions from the employee, and the employer may deduct amounts they contribute to the plan in their income for that year). Often these retirement plans are matched by the employer.

The markets do what the markets do; they go up and they go down. When the markets are up, funds are purchased at a higher price; when the market is down, the price of the funds is reduced. It's called Dollar Cost Averaging and works well when one is employed and the paychecks roll in week after week.

Some funds you may have just saved or maybe inherited, maybe you sold some property at a gain, etc. These are not tax-deferred but taxed normally as a short-term or long-term capital gain. There is a *big* difference in the tax treatment for capital gains and ordinary income. Understanding this can help to place you in a zero-tax category, if properly planned. Now, you can be like all the big guys (Microsoft, SalesForce, etc.).

You did all of this to build a nest-egg for when the income stopped coming in from working and you entered the Distribution Stage of your life. Now, you spend what you carefully saved and *that* must last you the rest of your life. We always plan for 30 years for a healthy 65-year-old male and longer for a woman of the same age.

In retirement, this changes.
Now, you must pay careful attention. There are two major factors:
RMDs and market volatility.

Your Tax-Deferred Accounts, A Tax Time-bomb

David Royer, author of *Top Ten IRA Mistakes*, speaks to navigating the retirement maze. One of the most important concepts to be aware of is that your IRA is yours and yours alone. I've got some very bad news for you. You have a partner and it's not your spouse. It's your Uncle Sam. He will determine and dictate when you pay the taxes on the IRA and how much you will pay.

David tells us that the second misconception is that you can beat the tax. The contract you have with the IRS is one that cannot be broken and there is not an out-clause. Even when you die, your uncle will get his share (your beneficiaries will be taxed). Again, the IRS will decide when you or your beneficiaries will pay the tax, and how much (percentage) will be taxed. Your uncle never loses or sleeps.

Think about it like this…you want to borrow some money for that boat you've dreamed of owning. You go to your local credit union and sit with a lender. You show her the pictures of the boat, the survey, and the sales price. You have 30% down (the boat is $100,000) and you need to finance the balance.

The loan officer tells you your credit is great and the value of the boat is good also. You are scheduled to have a closing over the weekend.

She says, "How would you like the funds, deposited in your account or a cashier's check?"

In your account will be fine, you tell her.

She says, "OK," and reaches out to shake your hand and as she does so, she says, "I'll have my assistant draw up the loan documents."

You are ready to shake her hand, but you draw back. You think to yourself *We never discussed interest rates or payback terms.* So, you hesitate, look up at her outstretched hand and into her eyes and say, "Marsha, aren't we forgetting some details on this loan?"

"What do you mean?" she asks.

You reply, "Well, what is the interest rate and term?" This is pretty important.

She pulls back her hand, takes a deep breath, and replies, "Oh, those details. Well, let me share the terms of this loan with you."

You sit back in your seat and carefully watch her face. You have researched these kinds of loans and you should come in around 5-8%. You're hoping for the lower rates.

Then she says, "You have great credit, you've been a longtime customer of the bank and we value your family and our relationship. We want to serve you. We're just not sure at this time of rate and terms. Tell you what, take the loan and when we need the money back, we'll let you know the rate and terms."

What the heck? No one would borrow that way. No one would have a partner without knowing what the costs are. What if the bank's "need" for money is greater when they want you to repay? What if the term is two years and not the seven you envisioned? What if the bank wants 20% interest?

You clearly are not comfortable with these terms and the complete loss of control in the situation. You tell Marsha, "Let me think about this and I'll get back to you." Of course, you would never borrow money without understanding and having a contract in place that spells out exactly what the terms are. No one would do this.

But that's exactly what your IRA or 401(k) has done for you. It's exactly what your partner, your favorite Uncle Sam, has dictated as the terms for withdrawals from your tax-deferred accounts. Yes, the tax on these accounts was *deferred* until you withdraw, but you have no say or control over what that tax will be. What actually happened here is that your uncle postponed the taxation on your account, and more importantly, he postponed the *calculation* of that taxation.

Let that sink in for a minute…

Required Minimum Distributions (RMDs)

You were a careful steward. You saved, you did without, you made sure your company had a match on the deferred accounts and you carefully tended the "garden" of your finances. The day has finally arrived when you can move from the Accumulation phase into the Distribution phase of your carefully-thought-out saving strategy that would allow you to start using this tax-deferred account to replace your paycheck.

But, there's a little problem. What if Congress and the IRS decide (and they can with the wave of a pen) to change the taxation on these accounts? What if they make changes to the tax code that mean you have to take out more than you calculated *and* pay a higher tax than you had planned?

Could that change your retirement plan? You bet it could and the chances that taxes will increase, maybe even double, are a better than even bet.

David McKnight, author of *The Power of Zero,* and the movie of the same name, (now available to view on our website at *www.LionsGateAdvisors.com/ThePowerOfZero)* warns us of a sovereign debt crisis unlike we have ever faced in this country. It explains in simple terms that the zero-sum mathematics we all learned in elementary school still apply—even to government. A city, county, state, country or a household simply cannot spend more than they make for long and have it all work out OK; 2+2=4 and $23 trillion in debt + another $3 trillion in debt still = $26 trillion in debt.

In the U.S., we are like college students on free beer night.

Spending is out of control and we simply don't collect enough revenue (taxes) to make up the deficit. This is not a Democratic or Republican Party issue, it's a MATH issue. And, we are sitting with our heads in the sand, merrily going about our business. Math does not lie and the crisis will catch up with us sooner than we may think.

So, what do we do?

You may believe that a politician would never raise taxes. It would be their doom. Remember, George H.W. Bush? *Read my lips.*

The other part of this formula is not just that at any time they want they can raise the rate of taxes on your deferred taxation retirement accounts, but they can unilaterally decide *when* you have to take withdrawals from those accounts.

What if you don't need the income from those retirement accounts right then? After all, you have Social Security, a nice pension and some savings. You live frugally and you have no debt.

Well, your uncle gets to decide that too. He came up with a special treatment of those retirement accounts that demands (with 50% plus the taxation penalty) you take a scheduled payment from those accounts *even* if they have gone down in value. Then, he makes sure you pay the income tax, at whatever he says the tax rate is when you withdraw. Your partner, Uncle Sam, makes all those decisions. You thought it was your hard-earned retirement savings, but, whether you knew it or not, you truly have a partner and he's hungry for tax dollars. You're his target and he's coming after you.

On the other hand, the pandemic has caused the government to roll out some changes to deferred taxation plans that are very positive. There is no RMD requirement for 2020 and a provision allows one to borrow from a 401(k) without penalty during the crisis.

RMDs – The new SECURE Act of 2019, *Setting Every Community Up for Retirement Enhancement*, is a far-reaching bill that includes 29 provisions aimed at increasing access to tax-advantaged accounts and preventing older Americans from outliving their assets. (In the appendix, you will find details on the SECURE Act of 2019).

In Chapter 11 we will show you ways you can take back control and mitigate some of these tax issues, and how to get the most out of these important tax-deferred accounts you have so carefully built.

The SECURE Act of 2019 is a good demonstration of what the government can do that actually addresses the needs of many in a timely manner.

Small businesses are offered tax incentives to enroll their employees in retirement plans. By allowing small businesses to "band together" in those plans, it encourages participation. Additionally, by eliminating the maximum age cap on contributions to retirement plans, it may help some to defer more of their earnings and build a retirement nest-egg for the longer life expectancy we now see as a real possibility. Also, one may now have annuities within their 401(k). This can really eliminate the downside of equity-based 401(k)s with solutions that have guarantees and offer lifetime income when activated.

The bill also raised the age for RMDs to 72 from 70-½. For those who have good pensions and other fixed income in retirement, this is good. Their IRAs can now grow another two years before withdrawals must occur.

On a not-so-bright side, the Stretch IRA provisions were eliminated, forcing the recipient of a no-spousal inherited IRA to take it over a maximum of 10 years. There are no RMDs for those 10 years, but it must all be withdrawn (balance and earnings) by the end of the tenth year. This would mean potentially boosting the tax burden on these accounts.

The Lion's Roar:
Key Takeaways from Chapter 7

- It is important to ensure that a portfolio is truly non-correlated, because if all the assets in a portfolio are correlated, they all rise (or drop!) at the same rate and time.
- The taxes due on your tax-deferred accounts are determined by the government and subject to changes in legislation.
- One thing is certain, there will be change. Keep connected and understand how to use these changes to your benefit.

SECTION II

Purpose, Plan, Progress

CHAPTER 8

THE PROCESS

Pinpoint the Problem – Ken & Karrie's First Meeting
You've done everything right. You paid your own way through college (your family wasn't wealthy, but you had pretty much what you needed growing up), you found a great mate and after your graduation, you were married. Two years later, your first child arrived. Your engineering degree (and that of your spouse) served you well. You both got positions in the aeronautical sector. Although your companies merged over the years, you really enjoy your jobs and the work is fascinating.

You put in 40 years and you took advantage of every possibility to save and utilize the deferred taxation opportunities, 401(k), and because you began your employment in the early 1970s, you have a pension. Your spouse, who took some time off to stay at home with the kids when they were young, doesn't have a pension, but you both have a cash balance plan. Your company allows you to take the company annuity pension or a buy-out with a lump sum dispersal—tax deferred, of course.

You also are a careful saver/spender, and you accumulated a nice nest-egg of non-qualified funds (not tax deferred) and when your parents died, they left you a tidy inheritance. Your spouse's parents are still living, although in an assisted living center. Dad has had some pretty difficult times and his memory, lately, seems to be a bit sketchy. It could be Alzheimer's or at best, early dementia. They have a small savings and with their Social Security and pensions just enough to pay the assisted living center, their health care deductibles, and Medigap insurance premiums. If Dad needs to go to a memory care facility or have stepped-up care, the money really isn't there. Your wife's siblings are not in a position to help financially. If Mom and Dad need assistance, you probably will have to be the ones.

Both kids are doing very well. Robbie, a software engineer, works for Amazon in Seattle, and Roberta is in her third year of residency after medical school and will soon be employed by a regional hospital not far from home as an OB/GYN. Neither is married and you are hoping for grandchildren someday.

You are proud of them both and pleased that you were able to have them finish their schooling with no student loan debt. They have great lives ahead!

Over the years you've done some of your own investing, playing with the stock market and sometimes you hit a great buy. More often than not, the results were mixed at best. Your 401(k) had limited options and the "kid" they sent over each year to meet with the group was a constantly changing face. It's almost like repping the fund each year is the scut-work investment firms save for their newbies. The choices were limited and, walking away from the conversation, you were never really sure how you picked your positions or why.

But that was OK; the last 10 years after the "correction" of 2007-9 had been good to your plan. It seemed pretty easy to get great returns no matter what you chose. Sure, the markets correct, but they always come back, don't they? And your financial planner at Schwab told you that, "you're in for the long run," and that these corrections are "healthy" ones. And, the best one of all, "it's only a loss on paper." It seems all financial salespeople parrot this advice. Did they all have the same coach?

As an engineer, you live in spreadsheets and, man, have you made a great one for your retirement. You're pretty sure you thought of everything, but what if you missed something?

Looking for ways to keep your brain active during the first year of retirement, you were browsing through a catalog from the University of Missouri Osher Lifelong Learning (classes for adult learners) and you saw one on financial planning—***Tax-Free Retirement***—and you thought that might be an interesting class. So, you signed up, took the two-night class, and walked away a bit puzzled about what you thought you knew to be true.

I mean, taxes will be less in retirement, right? Sovereign debt crisis? Not in this country, but the instructor had some pretty compelling, hard to explain facts; U.S. national debt over $23 trillion and something he called "Unfunded Liabilities" approaching $112 trillion. He pulled up a website, www.USDebtClock.org . The "clock" ran in real time and it was quite sobering to watch the debt grow faster than one could even see the wheels turn. It showed, in real time, spending and the income of the U.S. and compared it to other countries. The U.S. national debt was not just huge, but the debt per taxpayer was estimated to be $190,528. Per person!

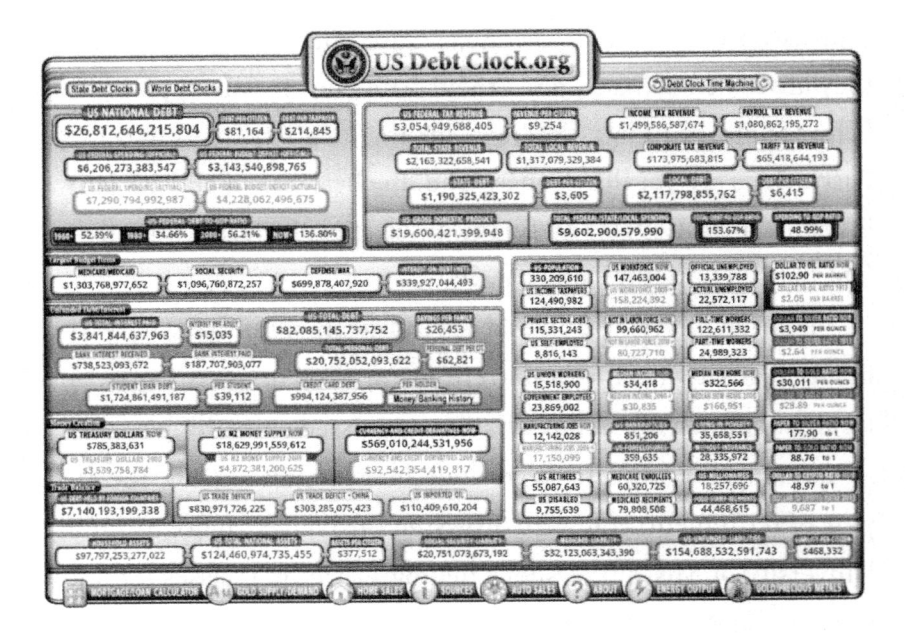

You left the class that day feeling a bit of panic. As an engineer, you had been able to control so much. You used the diagnostic approach and numbers and math did not lie. Now, the numbers the instructor showed you (also math) and the lack of control you had over the spending of the government made you almost feel queasy as you explained the concepts to your spouse.

Were you the tax time-bomb the instructor talked about? You had done everything right. Right? In the four hours of course lectures, you scribbled notes and when you got home you spent a lot more time on the spreadsheet. You had to admit, you were concerned.

The course instructor offered a "lab portion" of the course where you had the opportunity to visit his office and do a financial wellness checkup, just to verify that you had done everything right. So, you scheduled for a slot a week out and gathered your tax returns, financial statements, Social Security reports, wills, and trusts.

Getting your suit jacket out of the closet again, you wonder what he'll say? You don't really want to make any big changes, maybe a few small tweaks, but he'll surely notice what a good job you did on the spreadsheet. Won't he?

THE LIONSGATE PROCESS
PINPOINT

Ken & Karrie's situation is pretty much what we see every day in our offices and now on Zoom calls. We work with affluent and ultra-affluent families and businesses that have done well. They're comfortable, confident, and looking forward to retirement.

During the ***Diagnosis*** portion of the first meeting, we ask you questions that I have no doubt few if any financial planners have ever considered. The typical FP script goes as follows: "Where are your assets?" "What is the return?" Lastly, they always say, "We can do better."

We begin each new meeting with these questions:
- Where are you from and what was it like growing up?
- What did you learn about money growing up?
- What is the hardest lesson you've had to learn about money?
- What was the best experience you've had with money?
- What would you do with your time if no one paid you?
- What's on your mind today and why did you come?

After gaining a better understanding of how money influenced your life and the decisions you make, we begin the process of **Pinpointing** what you have done to get you to this place in your life. We look at your tax return, we ask questions about what your expected expenses are in retirement, where is your income coming from and what are your **Needs, Wants, and Wishes**?

In order to Pinpoint a successful retirement, we need to find clear and collectively understood goals. Will you be traveling? House remodel? Buy a vacation home? Weddings ahead for children? Do you have a special needs child or grandchild in the family? Will you want to contribute to the education expenses of any grands? What steps have you taken for expenses related to aging parents and what about your possible needs for extended care? Do you have discretionary income? Where are your current investments and what is your necessary risk compared to your needs? Are your portfolios in line with those risks and needs? Is there portfolio disconnect? Are you unnecessarily paying too much in taxes? Could that be mitigated? What is your estate plan? Are your assets protected from probate?

What if taxes double?

Only once we have taken this discovery time to Pinpoint your situation, *can we begin to calculate the costs of not changing any of your retirement tactics.*

Calculate

Let me give you an example. We met with a couple who had worked for a large American energy company; they were a referral from one of our very happy families. During the Discovery/Pinpoint process in the first meeting, we took a look at their tax return—your IRS report card—and saw some pretty glaring items that could mean they were paying more in taxes than was necessary.

Below is an example of an IRS return (Chart 5); 3a and 3b are where dividends are reported. In this family's case, Qualified Dividends were $15,000 and Ordinary Dividends were $84,000. You might say, that's great, we all like dividends. But, the tax treatment of Qualified versus Ordinary Dividends is very different. Ordinary Dividends are treated as Ordinary Income and Qualified Dividends as a Capital Gain, either long term or short term. So, the tax for this client on his $84,000 in Ordinary Dividends was at about 45% with Federal and State taxes, $37,800! Of that great dividend of $84,000, he got to keep $46,200 and his Uncle Sam got the rest!

If the dividends had been Qualified ones, he would have paid a Long-Term Capital Gain of 26%: 20% Federal and 6% state, based on his high Adjusted Gross Income (AGI) of $600,000. That's a big difference! In this example, it is $15,960 for that year. What if it happened over and over, year after year for the next 25 years of your retirement? I'll calculate it for you. It's $398,750. Isn't there something you'd rather do with $400k than to give it to your Uncle Sam? And, I'll bet he won't even send you a thank-you card.

Now, the question is, "Do you want to fix it?"

Contrast

And, that's what we call the **Contrast** portion of your diagnosis. Can you imagine? This is just one small, short line on a tax return that in most cases, financial salespeople never look over, never take into consideration, and never make a part of your analysis. Did your accountant talk to you about this in January to plan for the next year's taxation? It's doubtful.

The vast majority of accountants are historians, adept at the filing of taxes but not so proactive in creating strategies for tax mitigation.

It's not their job, they believe. Your financial salesperson certainly is not very interested in this. I mean, she gets paid on assets under management, so, the more the better.

What if there were four or five ways to mitigate taxes and each one saved you a small amount yearly? What would that look like after 25 years? What we find in most cases is that families have some tactics they may have developed for retirement over the years, but no real complete strategy.

Then, when we begin the discussion about Legacy, the hard questions come out.

At LionsGate Advisors, we are not accountants or estate attorneys, but we have put together an integrated resource network of the best advisors in each field.

It looks like this:

Estate/Trust Planning
Tax Planning
Retirement Income Planning
Asset Management
Extended Term Care

Or, we can work with your current trusted advisors to coordinate the tactics and strategies.

So, now it just comes down to a few simple questions after the Diagnostic process:

1. Are you SATISFIED?
2. Are you AWARE?
3. Do you want to FIX it?
4. What are your OPTIONS?

Ken's Concerns

Returning to Ken and Karrie's initial meeting with the LionsGate Advisory team, the coffee and fresh cookies had been served. The Privacy and Security agreement had been signed, assuring these potential clients that their information would be securely looked after. The couple started walking us through the main reason for seeking us out.

"What brings you in today?" the planners asked.

Ken began to answer by telling the story of their recent retirement, the class he attended and the warning signs he saw in the economy of the U.S. and the world. "I'm not an economist, but trying to filter the bias out of the comments made by talking heads on TV, and what I read in the news makes me more than a little nervous."

It all came down to one main concern. Taxes. After the class, Ken had a new awareness about taxes. Yes, he understood the inevitability of paying them, but he wasn't prepared to pay a higher rate after retirement than before. He had always believed that taxes and expenses would go down in their retirement years. Now, six months into their new life, he was beginning to see that expenses would not go down. They traveled more and had more free time on their hands, and that often meant more spending.

Sure, their income was less, but he was already thinking about the taxes in this first year of retirement. He realized they would not have the deductions for the 401(k)s and now that the house was paid off, one of their goals for retirement, they no longer had the interest deduction on the mortgage. Both kids were on their own, no deduction there. Health care now was their biggest expense. Sure, they had Medicare, but still had to pay deductibles and Medigap insurance costs.

Most of all, he recently read David McKnight's book, *The Power of Zero*. That reading along with the class about taxes had really changed his thinking about the impending sovereign debt crisis and what measures they could take to mitigate some of the taxes they would have to pay.

"And what about our Required Minimum Distributions?" Ken asked, his forehead wrinkling with concern. "How will they impact our retirement accounts? They're in the market, you know. When the markets correct—and I believe they will do so multiple times in the coming years—what's going to happen to our thirty-year plan?"

When Ken and Karrie had interviewed other potential financial planners, they'd seemed nice enough. But nice wasn't going to help them protect their hard-earned assets from potentially ruinous tax burdens. Neither of the other two firms had asked any questions about taxes, and now Ken knew that to be dangerous and was concerned.

To Ken's relief, the LionsGate team next asked if he'd brought his last two tax returns. He had and as they examined them, made some notes, they expressed what Ken already knew, that this first year in retirement would make the tax year look a lot different. They said there were some proactive measures that could be taken to begin reducing future taxes, and that would be a topic of discussion if Ken and Karrie became clients.

The team at the table asked about savings, 401(k)s, pensions, Social Security, property, and expenses. How many trips did they anticipate taking each year and at what costs? How often did they buy cars? What did they think a wedding for Roberta would cost? What were their Needs, Wants, and Wishes? Would Karrie's parents need financial assistance as they aged?

They then went to the whiteboard and did a bit of drawing, showing the two a chart divided into four quadrants: *Income, Assets, Cash Reserve, Legacy*. Looking through the stack of financial statements, they categorized each. Income included Ken and Karrie's pension and Social Security. *Assets* were all of their retirement accounts and the inherited money. *Cash* was cash; it was determined that they probably had too much of it in money market accounts. Finally, *Legacy* included their house and the two Roth accounts they had carefully contributed to until their salaries were too great to allow.

The advisor drawing on the board next drew three circles. Ken remembered that from class: *Taxable, Tax Deferred,* and *Tax Free*. When the advisor was through drawing on the board and placing the dollar amounts in each bucket, there was a pause and he asked, "What do you see here that might cause you some alarm?"

Karrie and Ken looked to the board and back at each other. They remembered the class and this part well. It was what made them make the decision to come to LionsGate for the financial checkup. The words came out of both their mouths at exactly the same time, "Tax Time-bomb!" They looked to the board again and then to each other's eyes and grinned. Yes, being married 35 years made you alike in so many ways.

The advisors at LionsGate wrapped up this meeting by briefly discussing another topic covered in the class, that of a Fiduciary and the best interest for the client.

Another slide in the deck showed a wheel with LionsGate in the center and what they called "trusted advisors" along the border of the wheel.

Diagram: Five ovals arranged around a central lion logo — Estate/Trust Planning, Tax Planning, Retirement Income Planning, Asset Management, Extended Term Care.

LionsGate explained that they were not attorneys or CPAs, but would "quarterback" and focus the work of these advisors to make sure each family was covered in each area and that all the advisors were working together as a team.

Ken and Karrie loved this concept. At the aeronautical plant, they had worked in teams, and accomplishments went up directly and proportionately to how well those teams functioned.

Ken and Karrie made the decision to meet again with LionsGate, and set an appointment to go over the Diagnostics that the team would go through in the next meeting.

Some Thoughts About the Fiduciary Standard
When we engage the services of an attorney or a CPA or a physician, we don't even consider that they have anything but our best

interest in the advice they give to us. In fact, each of these is legally required to act in the best interests of the people they help. Financial advisors are not. Read that again.

Unlike doctors, attorneys, or CPAs, financial advisors are not legally required to act in the best interest of their clients.

Yet, in his book, *Unshakeable: Your Financial Freedom Playbook – Creating Peace of Mind in a World of Volatility,* Tony Robbins reports, "From 2010-2015, the percentage of Americans using financial advisors doubled. In fact, more than 40% of Americans now use an advisor. And the more money you have, the more likely you are to seek out advice: 81% of people with more than $5 million have an advisor."

While the use of financial advisors is rising, trust in them isn't doing the same. The **Certified Financial Planner Board of Standards** conducted a survey in 2016 and found that 60% of respondents "believe that financial advisors act in their companies' best interests rather than the consumers' best interests." ("Participant Trust and Engagement Study," National Association of Retirement Plan Participants, 2016). It raises the question, why.

We've been programmed to trust multinational names like Bank of America, JPMorgan Chase, Citigroup, Wells Fargo, BNP, Paribas, UBS, Deutsche Bank, Morgan Stanley, Barclays and Credit Suisse; however, these same suspects have been hit with fines and agreed to settlements amounting to $179.5 billion in just the seven years spanning 2009-2015. We may need to adjust our thinking and begin to ask more questions.

Only 10% of Americans surveyed TRUST financial institutions.

One might think these large fines would act as some kind of deterrent, but based on their lack of course correction, these penalties are clearly chump change. Bank of America had to pay $415 million for misusing its customers' assets. Yet, in one three-month period in 2015, this bank earned a profit of $5.3 billion! They aren't shaking in their boots.

Take a peek at your monthly retirement statements; whose names are printed on the letterhead? For many, it's one of the names above or one of the same ilk. We are asked to place our trust and retirement security in the hands of an industry that has demonstrated without fail that it places its interests above those of their clients. They are too big to fail and they maximize profits above all else.

So, who do you trust? Your brother's guy? He does take him to play golf a couple of times a year, drives a Mercedes, and has a great office. How about my uncle, I mean after all he is family!

Obviously, I'm joking to make a point. It *is* confusing and it may be purposefully so.

The *Wall Street Journal* reported in 2019 that there are 208 different designations for financial advisors!

Some better-known ones include: Advisor, Financial Advisor, Financial Planner, Registered Representative (RR), Financial

Consultant, Wealth Manager, Insurance Agent, CFP – Certified Financial Planner, CFA – Certified Financial Analyst, ChFC – Chartered Financial Consultant, CFS – Certified Fund Specialist, CIMA – Certified Investment Management Analyst, CMT – Chartered Market Technician—and the list goes on and on.

Mindy Diamond, CEO of Diamond Consultants, wrote March 5, 2019 in *WealthManagement.com*, "While wire house advisors may have every intention of acting as a fiduciary and making decisions with their clients' best interests in mind, the very nature of working for a big brokerage firm often makes it impossible for them to do so."

I agree with Mindy Diamond. Financial planners and others in that class often find themselves in conflict between the clients' best interests and profit—both individual profit and company profit (meaning pressure from the boss). Because their fee comes from sales commissions on products they recommend, one has to take their advice with a grain of salt. It's a huge conflict of interest, and it's the reason behind the lack of public trust.

The issue here is that there are two different regulatory standards that professionals can abide by, the Fiduciary Standard and the Suitability Standard. A licensed Fiduciary, such as an RIA (Registered Investment Advisor), has a legal obligation to act in the client's best interest. Conversely, brokers and insurance agents (who frequently use pseudonyms such as financial representative or consultant, registered representative, client or wealth advisor) are held to a lesser measure called the Suitability Standard, which simply requires the broker to sell investments they believe are suitable for their clients, not necessarily what is best for the client.

Obviously, I'm biased; however, there are some clear differences between the two classes that you should know about.

1. Freedom to Act in the Best Interest of the Client
It can't be overstated that when clients meet with a non-fiduciary, they are meeting with a salesperson. That's not to say that folks in this side of the industry are bad, or out to get you. Not at all. They do, however, answer to someone besides their clients. So, even if their intention is to serve clients, the first stop must always be the big boss upstairs.

Here's an example. When my partner Jonathan worked at a large brokerage, he attended a big convention right before the markets all started melting down in 2001. Attendees were told that market corrections were likely coming soon and they could be big, possibly by as much as 40-50%. But they were forbidden from telling clients about this forecast. When Jonathan ignored that edict and tried to alert clients that they might want to convert at least some assets to cash, he got fired. Even though that would have protected people from losses, the brokerage wasn't making money on cash in portfolios.

Speaking of portfolios, here's another way fiduciary clients get the best advice. We often see clients in their eighties who are using the same portfolio strategy that they started out with in their twenties. Why? Because the planners they used didn't consider the whole wide world of possible options for them. They instead suggested the same cookie-cutter strategy they were selling to all their other clients.

And who can blame them? If I'm a broker-dealer and my client has three to four million to invest, I'm not going to recommend moving half those funds to life insurance because I won't make any commission on that. As a fiduciary advisor, I can suggest to that same 80-year-old to move those funds to a life insurance plan. That works to benefit heirs, to manage tax burdens, and especially because it's in the best interest of my client to have a more diversified portfolio. Because my fees aren't tied to transactions, I have no incentive to steer people toward plans that could be risky for them. Instead I can teach them how to evolve their investment strategies as their lives change.

2. Transparency

Fiduciaries are required to disclose all the fees involved in working with them. Because of the Series 65 license they hold, fiduciaries are the only advisors who can charge a flat plan fee, or fees for managing the value of a portfolio, unlike stockbrokers or dealers. So, going in, clients know up front exactly how much it will cost to work with firms like ours.

If, for example, I recommend life insurance, I must disclose any prior relationship with partnering companies. The SEC and FINRA make us reveal that as a part of doing business.

Our regular audits from FINRA and the SEC include deep dives into our process. Fiduciaries must be able to prove a standardized procedure that is the same for every client. (Remember Ken and Karrie's Discovery, Needs/Wants/Wishes, and Pinpoint meetings? We do that for everyone). *Plus,* we have to justify why we made recommendation A over B and how that was the best option for that client. That's what is meant by the Fiduciary Standard.

A Shift in Dynamics

There's a shift in the dynamics of the wealth management space—it's becoming less about one model versus another and more about the ability of advisors to play enhanced roles in their clients' lives.

Mark Tibergien, CEO of BNY Mellon Pershing Advisor Solutions, explained on a recent LionsGate Advisors podcast episode. "When we look at those who are breaking away and forming their own firms, we recognize that they're making a fundamental change from being an employee to being a business owner, from being a broker to being a fiduciary advisor and from being a product advocate to being a client advocate."

Ultimately, a fiduciary operates without conflict and with one driving force: the client's best interests. As this sentiment among advisors grows, it will continue to serve as one of the most significant catalysts for migration to the independent space.

Tony Robbins in his book, *Unshakeable*, goes on to say, "Regardless of the title, what you really need to know is that 90% of the roughly 310,000 financial advisors in America are just brokers. In other words, they're paid to sell financial products to customers like you and me in return for a fee."

So, let's take a look at the three categories 90% of financial planners fall into.

- Broker
- IAR– Investment Advisor Representative - independent advisor
- Dually registered advisor

Statistics show us that of the 310,000 financial advisors, only 5,000 are pure fiduciaries. I'll do the math for you on that. It's 1.6%.

To find that small group of advisors who operate solely for their clients' interests, go to www.brokercheck.com and check the credentials of your potential advisor before signing anything. A Series 65 licensee is the only true fiduciary. A dually is one who holds a Series 65, a Series 7, maybe a Series 6, or Series 66 or Series 63.

Michael A Webb, CEBS of Carmack Retirement, wrote an article September 2019 on how to check out your advisor or potential advisor at *brokercheck.com*, a FINRA resource.

> "By entering an individual advisor or firm's name, a user can immediately determine whether he/she/it is a Registered Investment Adviser (a higher fiduciary standard), a Broker-Dealer (lower suitability standard), or both. Colored circles, labeled "IA" for Investment Adviser and "B" for Brokerage Firm, immediately and easily identify the firms and individuals. And then, by clicking on that entity's Investment Adviser and Broker Dealer box (or boxes, for firms with more than one registered name, active or inactive), users gain access to a whole host of easily accessible information."

Webb's article continues by explaining that the FINRA (an independent, non-governmental watchdog firm) website takes users directly to the SEC's page when they click on any Investment Advisor bio. This is because IAs are regulated by this higher-clearance commission, and maintain records of any disciplinary actions, assets under management, number of employees, etc. Access this information by looking for an advisor's Form ADV or Part 2 Brochure.

Also on the FINRA site, you can find information about Broker-Dealers. Webb explains further:

"For Broker-Dealers, it is even less work to find the info you want. After clicking on a "B" box, users are immediately taken to a page where there is a box titled "Disclosures." If the number in that box is "0," the firm or individual has had no customer complaints or arbitrations, regulatory actions, employment terminations, bankruptcy filings, or civil or criminal proceedings against them that were required to be disclosed in their FINRA file. If there is a number in that box, they have had such disclosures, and users can quickly scroll down and click on the 'detailed report' link which will provide details in a complete BrokerCheck report."

Finding out exactly who is quarterbacking your team is vital if you are to have a strategy and written plan that will last the possible 30 years you will have in retirement. You need someone experienced and unbiased when considering the complex tax and estate issues at stake. Be careful; a mistake here could be a serious one that could have long-lasting repercussions.

A Few Thoughts on Risk Tolerance
Markets go up and they go down. It's just a fact of life. What's not random is how much of that up and down action you're willing to expose yourself to, aka risk tolerance.

Risk tolerance is how emotionally comfortable a person is with taking financial risk. For example, how much a person is willing for their portfolio to diminish for a chance to make bigger returns. It is psychological and is best measured with a psychometric tool.

When financial advisors put together a plan, they attempt to do so in accordance with the risk tolerance of their client in mind. Thus, every financial advisor you've ever worked with has likely administered some sort of quiz to learn how emotionally comfortable you are with financial unpredictability.

Because this is a psychological measure, it's pretty subjective, especially if the quiz is designed to steer toward a suitability standard, not a fiduciary standard. In other words, a quiz that lands you in one of three buckets, conservative, moderate, or aggressive, is oversimplified. Then, when an advisor looks at that score and decides on strategies based on the answers to that one quiz, they're using a non-nuanced tool to make a subjective call. What's conservative to you might be aggressive to me. Or vice versa.

Not all risk-profiling tools are created equally; some tools are better at delivering measurable results than others. At LionsGate, we prefer an Australian tool called FinaMetrica that helps get both clients and their advising team to a finely tuned understanding of goals and potential outcomes.

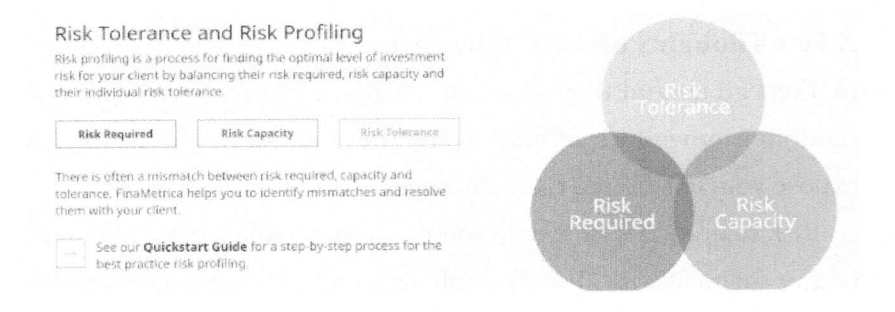

Risk Tolerance and Risk Profiling

Risk profiling is a process for finding the optimal level of investment risk for your client by balancing their risk required, risk capacity and their individual risk tolerance.

| Risk Required | Risk Capacity | Risk Tolerance |

There is often a mismatch between risk required, capacity and tolerance. FinaMetrica helps you to identify mismatches and resolve them with your client.

See our **Quickstart Guide** for a step-by-step process for the best practice risk profiling.

- **Risk Tolerance** – the level of financial risk the client is emotionally comfortable with.
- **Risk Required** - the risk associated with the return required to achieve the client's goals from the financial resources available.
- **Risk Capacity** – the level of financial risk the client can afford to take.

Risk Comfort (or risk tolerance) is an important measurement as we access our financial situation. The Risk Required is the level one must consider taking to achieve the goals (Needs, Wants and Wishes) for our retirement. Risk Capacity sets parameters on measurable and acceptable risk that one must take without causing the whole plan to implode in a market correction.

The Lion's Roar:
Key Takeaways from Chapter 8
- For many people, their taxes go up, not down in retirement years.
- One key wealth preservation strategy for retirees is shifting Ordinary Dividends into Qualified Dividends, thereby lowering the rate at which they are taxed.
- A fiduciary firm like LionsGate Advisors can help steer clients to savings that are based on their needs, wants, and wishes, not the goals of the financial planner.
- Understand your risk comfort level and make sure your plan is built around that number. Remember, change is inevitable; monitor your plan on a very regular basis to make sure it continues to be in alignment with your goals.

CHAPTER 9

ACCELERATING THE IMPACT OF YOUR WEALTH

The week between the first and second meeting at LionsGate seemed longer than usual. Karrie and Ken grew more anxious by the day to see what the team at LionsGate had uncovered in their diagnosis. It was not unlike waiting for test results from the doctor. Ken went over his spreadsheet every day to see if there was some glaring mistake he had made or something for which he had not accounted. He felt pretty good about the data and had sent a copy to the LionsGate team for them to analyze.

Wednesday rolled around and Ken and Karrie entered the office. They were met by Wilma, the Director of First Impressions as it said on her business card, and she immediately came out from her reception desk with a big smile and a sincere greeting. The aroma of freshly baked chocolate chip cookies was subtle but made Karrie visualize her grandmother's farmhouse when she was a kid. Every visit to Grandma's house was sure to include *something* mouthwatering. It wasn't quite that good at LionsGate, but it was inviting.

Wilma gave them both iPads and instructed them on completing a FinaMetrica Risk Tolerance questionnaire. It took about ten minutes, and in the meantime, out of the corner of her eye,

Karrie saw that two advisors were entering the conference room from their areas.

Just as they finished the risk tolerance questionnaire on the device, Jason appeared and greeted them with a warm smile while showing them to the conference room.

Ken's Narrative

Ken and Karrie sat down. The cookies and hot coffee were waiting as well as a pen and a pad upon which to write notes. No one seemed in a hurry; everyone took a moment to look around at the room, take a bite of the cookies and a sip of the warm, aromatic coffee.

What had they found?

Mark started off by reviewing their last meeting's agenda and conclusions. Ken's spreadsheet had been received and Mark asked, "Is there anything from the last meeting we need to cover in more depth now that you've had time to review everything?"

The work and notes from the last meeting were up on the interactive whiteboard.

Mark drew the three circles on the board as Jason had done in the class and also at the last meeting. Ken and Karrie were beginning to be pretty familiar with these.

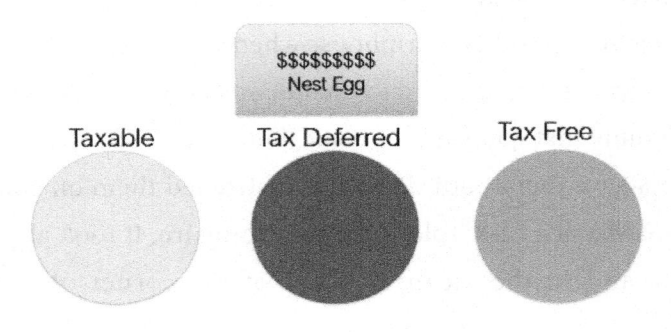

Then, he added Ken & Karrie's to their proper circles. After he finished drawing, it looked like this:

```
                    $$$$$$$$$$
                     Nest Egg

   Taxable          Tax Deferred         Tax Free

  $535k – Joint        IRA's              Roth
  $150k – MMA       $1.56mm Ken        $200k – Ken
  $35k – Checking   $750k Karrie       $200k – Karrie
                    $250k Inherited
```

Mark asked Ken first, "Is there anything here that alarms you or sends up a red flag?"

Ken felt like a kid back in school who'd studied hard before a test. He knew the answer, they had discussed it extensively in class; this was the tax time-bomb Jason had spent so much time defining. These were the accounts they had so carefully contributed to and watched as they grew over their working careers. These were the retirement accounts that were *supposed* to make sure their "golden years" were stress free and enjoyable. *And now they're telling me this is a tax time-bomb?*

Karrie said, "We've done well. We've been careful spenders and we have saved and saved. We took advantage of *every* deferred taxation program offered and now we are the poster child of what you taught in class!"

Ken knew from his spreadsheet that with their good pension, Social Security, and withdrawals they had to take from the inherited IRA, they had good income. "We can leave those IRAs pretty much alone...well, at least we won't have to withdraw until we turn seventy-two in seven years."

Mark added, "And what would that amount be at age seventy-two, Ken?"

Now Ken had another school-days emotion. This time, though, he was reminded of times he hadn't fully understood the material before the class discussion. Ken knew there was a complex formula for calculating RMDs but had not built it into the spreadsheet he had made.

"That's OK," Mark smiled. "That formula is kinda tricky." Mark shared that if the $2.5mm deferred-taxation accounts grew at 5.6% over the next seven years, the worth would be close to $3.2mm and the RMD (if the government didn't change how they calculated it) would be $126k and grow each year in spite of the withdrawals. Of course, if there were a recession or correction, that would change. At age 82, they would be required to take out $206k a year.

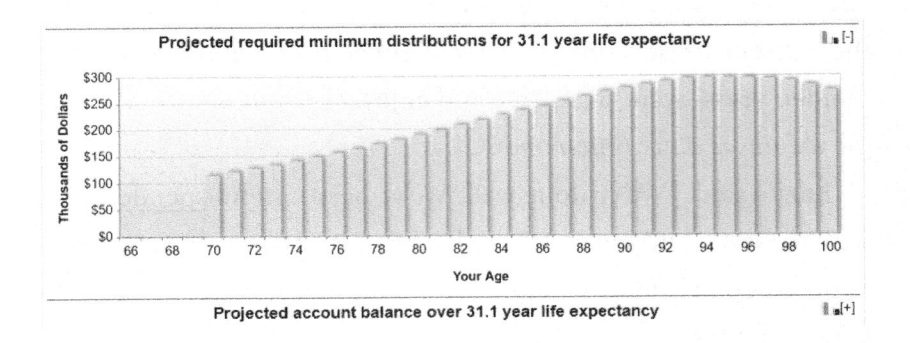

Projected required minimum distributions for 31.1 year life expectancy

Projected account balance over 31.1 year life expectancy

Mark added, "By giving you the ability to save tax deferred all those years, Uncle Sam's real motive will come home to roost. They didn't tax the seed, but they will tax the crop, at whatever the rate might be at that point in time.

"Tax Deferred and Tax Postponed. Two words that seem so similar until you apply them in your life. Not only does your uncle give you the tax postponement, but he also postpones the ***tax calculation*** and that tax calculation could be much higher than the current rates. And, if you don't take your RMD withdrawals, he fines you an additional 50% of what the RMD amount would be *plus* the taxation on it. Your uncle always gets his share."

Ken and Karrie looked at each other, then back to the board and the drawings. The room was silent as it sank in. If tax rates doubled like David McKnight and the Congressional Budget Office predict they will, over half of their withdrawals could go to their Uncle Sam. Ken and Karrie are proud Americans, but that scenario seemed extreme. After all, they had done everything right. Now would they have to be the ones who pay?

"What can we do about this?" asked Karrie.

Jason replied, "We specialize in working with families like yours that have done everything right and want to pay their fair share of taxes, but not overpay. What you have is a good problem that is solvable with the right tactics, strategies, and coordination of advisors."

During the discussion, Blake had been working on "grading" their risk-tolerance survey they had taken on the iPad earlier. After explaining what risk tolerance really means to the family investor, he showed them the results.

Your risk tolerance is the degree of uncertainty you are willing to take on to achieve potentially greater rewards. The measure is determined by a set of questions that underscore your appetite for risk and reward. You (and your advisor) need to understand how much risk you're willing to take and which types of risks most worry you. Your risk tolerance is determined by a combination of factors, including your investment goals and experience, how much time you have to invest, your other financial resources and your "fear factor"—how freaked out you get by the capricious nature of the market.

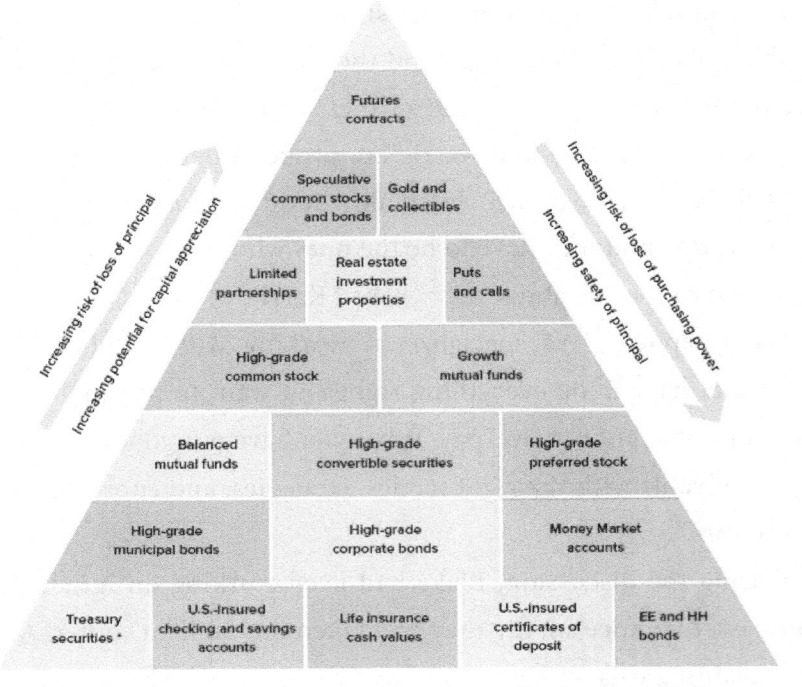

```
                        Futures
                       contracts

               Speculative
              common stocks      Gold and
               and bonds       collectibles

          Limited         Real estate        Puts
       partnerships       investment       and calls
                          properties

           High-grade                    Growth
          common stock               mutual funds

      Balanced          High-grade          High-grade
    mutual funds    convertible securities  preferred stock

     High-grade          High-grade         Money Market
   municipal bonds     corporate bonds        accounts

                 U.S.-insured                    U.S.-insured
   Treasury    checking and savings Life insurance certificates of   EE and HH
  securities*        accounts       cash values      deposit          bonds
```

Increasing risk of loss of principal / Increasing potential for capital appreciation

Increasing risk of loss of purchasing power / Increasing safety of principal

* If held to maturity. Otherwise, they are subject to volatility due to interest rate risk as with any other type of bond.

Equities, Bonds, Stocks, REITS, and other investments are "graded" in part by their volatility and risk tolerance. Generally, risk tolerance falls on a scale of 1-100. A grade of one equates to storing all your money under the mattress and 100 is akin to placing it on black at the roulette wheel. The continuum of risk looks like this. Less risky investments at the bottom of the pyramid are more liquid and offer stable (although lower) rates of return.

Ken's score was a 43 and Karrie's a 39.

Blake explained, "There is no 'right' score. We're not trying to steer you one way or another. This assessment is merely a tool that helps advisors to be able to select a portfolio and strategies that are consistent with the risk preference of each person; we average it for the family. So, in your case, your family risk preference would be forty-one. We then can test our recommendations against your goals to arrive at a suitable and best interest recommendation. Remember Needs, Wants, and Wishes?

"In the program we use to help determine your aversion to risk, there is a link analysis to a forty-plus years of month-by-month back testing of historical portfolio performance. At a glance, we can show you how representative sample portfolios would have performed against your risk and return expectations."

Ken and Karrie nodded confidently as they sipped more coffee.

Jason checked their expressions for understanding then continued. "In the course of our Discovery meeting last week, we asked you what you believed was a realistic and expected return in your mind, remember? You both said about five to six percent. We believe those are realistic numbers for a family that has done well and is entering retirement. If you had said ten to twelve percent, we would have communicated to you that in order to possibly receive these kinds of returns, one would have to take significantly more risk. And, is that merited in your case where you have good pensions, savings, and retirement funds?"

Ken and Karrie looked thoughtfully at the board and then down to the report on risk tolerance that Blake had handed to them. They were not risk takers, they had been careful all their lives, measuring their goals and work against unnecessary risk. They shook their heads no in answer to the question.

Now the board changed to a report that showed the positions in their current portfolio with a risk number attached to each fund or stock. Cash was a 1; most of their bonds scored between 5 and 20; and the equities ranged from 34-98. Overall, their average score was a 72.

"What does all this mean?" said Karrie.

Blake explained, "Your risk preference is one of about forty-one, but your investments overall show a risk of about seventy-two." He paused to let this sink in. "You are taking more risk than necessary to achieve your goals."

Ken and Karrie's brows wrinkled as they wondered how they had reached this undesirable outcome.

Jason then explained, "We call this 'portfolio disconnect,' where a family who has been in a growth pattern during working years, now needs to change to a preservation pattern with growth and income in retirement. Let me give you an example: when a woman is pregnant, she goes to what kind of doctor?"

Karrie replied, "Ob/gyn."

"Yes, and when the baby is born and for post-natal checkups, what kind of physician do we go to?"

"Pediatrician," said Karrie as she visualized the wonderful doctor who had helped her through the first years after Robbie was born. No one could have told her how difficult it was to see a newborn through the many illnesses they developed.

"And, then as we enter the teen years, we switch to…"

"Family medicine," replied Ken. His brother was a primary care physician and he knew that answer. His brother had seen the children through their teens and into college.

"And now that we've reached our retirement years, we see all kinds of doctors, right? Cardiology, gastroenterology, rheumatology, gerontology, and so on. If I get sick today, I don't go back to my pediatrician. That doesn't mean she's no longer a good doctor. I just need the right specialist for the job, the one who can address the changes in my body and knows how to diagnose and treat people with those situations because she does it every day.

"The same is true for your current broker; he is more of an accumulation specialist and when one retires, the focus must change. A paradigm shift must take place. It's not a matter of character, but one of specialty.

"Because our specialty is retired and close-to-retirement families, we focus on their unique situations. You're definitely not the only ones. We see this portfolio disconnect over and over again. Risk in the family portfolio is unnecessary to achieve the results needed, your Needs, Wants, and Wishes."

Ken sat back in his chair, carefully weighing Jason's words and ideas. He was starting to wonder how good that spreadsheet really was. He had calculated a 6% return over the 30 years of life expectancy.

Earlier in the meeting, Jason had asked about inflation and health care costs. He had explained that the average inflation from 2009–2020 was 1.9%. Yet, health care costs had risen significantly faster, to the tune of over 5%.

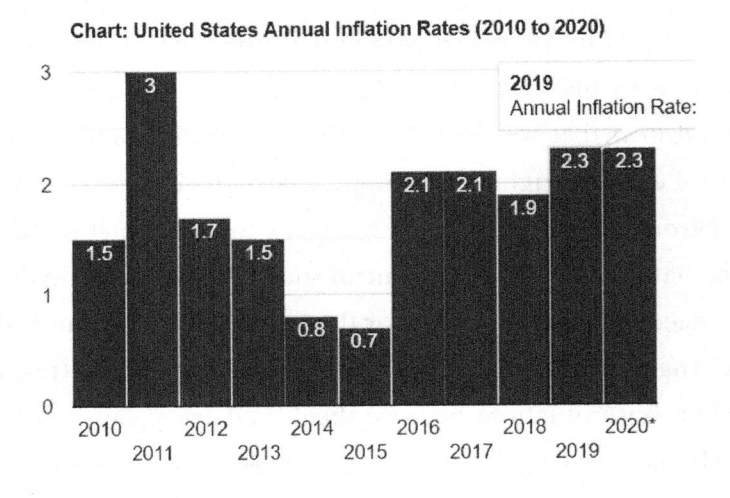

Chart: United States Annual Inflation Rates (2010 to 2020)

Year	Rate
2010	1.5
2011	3
2012	1.7
2013	1.5
2014	0.8
2015	0.7
2016	2.1
2017	2.1
2018	1.9
2019	2.3
2020*	2.3

2019 Annual Inflation Rate:

https://www.modernhealthcare.com/article/20181025/NEWS/181029946/healthcare-price-growth-significantly-outpaces-inflation

Jason referenced an article from *Modern Healthcare,* March 2020, where the disconnect was outlined:

> *Healthcare prices continue to rise across the country, according to a new study.*
>
> *Over a five-year period, healthcare prices increased in 111 out of 112 metro areas analyzed by the Healthcare Cost Institute. The*

outlier was Durham-Chapel Hill, N.C., where prices dropped 5% from 2012 to 2016, HCCI's analysis of 1.7 billion commercial healthcare claims showed.

Healthcare prices grew about 16% over that period, which was about three times the inflation rate, said Bill Johnson, the author of the report and senior researcher at HCCI.

"Prices aren't going down virtually anywhere, no matter where you are looking," he said.

Inside his head, Ken was thinking, *uh oh*. He had not figured rapid inflation into his spreadsheet and was now trying to figure out on the fly how that would change their numbers. Just as he was getting more into the internal dialogue, Jason spoke again.

"Part of our diagnosis process includes building out all the costs, including health care inflation, stress-test that to your Needs, Wants, and Wishes, and make sure you will cross the finish line in retirement successfully. As with the recent COVID-19 pandemic, the world changes and our job is to make sure you navigate through those changes. Remember the sailing story? When I sail across the ocean, we check our position numerous times daily. We make course corrections regularly, sometime small ones and sometimes they are more dramatic. So it is with retirement, Purpose, Plan, and Progress. As life changes, the course must be corrected.

"We have completed an initial diagnosis of where you are today, where you want to be in retirement, the current risks and volatility of your portfolios today, and after stress-testing all, we have a chart to share with you."

Mark jumped in (they really were a team; Karrie liked that) and shared how a "stress test" worked.

"We use what is called a Monte Carlo Risk Analysis. Risk analysis is part of every decision we make. A Monte Carlo Simulation lets an investor see the possible outcomes of decisions we make and assess the impact of risk."

On the board, Mark brought up an article by Palisade which explained the history of this simulation.

What is Monte Carlo Simulation?

Monte Carlo simulation is a computerized mathematical technique that allows people to account for risk in quantitative analysis and decision making. The technique is used by professionals in such widely disparate fields as finance, project management, energy, manufacturing, engineering, research and development, insurance, oil & gas, transportation, and the environment.

Monte Carlo simulation furnishes the decision-maker with a range of possible outcomes and the probabilities they will occur for any choice of action. It shows the extreme possibilities—the outcomes of going for broke and for the most conservative decision—along with all possible consequences for middle-of-the-road decisions.

The technique was first used by scientists working on the atom bomb; it was named for Monte Carlo, the Monaco resort town renowned for its casinos. Since its introduction in World War II, Monte Carlo simulation has been used to model a variety of physical and conceptual systems.

Mark explained, "We run situations through a thousand different scenarios: sequence of return, up years, down years, inflation high, low, etc. The algorithms determine your chances for success. For our families, we want to see an 85-99% score.

"To put it into simple terms, if you had to get into a canoe on one side of the lake early one morning and then begin to cross the lake from sunup to sunset, a thousand times, and the environment was constantly changing, wind, currents, boats flying by, you would find out how many times you would be successful. You would want the curve to fall somewhere in the ninety-percentile range. You would not like to take too many dunks in the cold water. This is what we do with this simulation."

They then showed Ken and Karrie a chart—see appendix.

Ken stared at the slide and thought *They did exactly what they promised they would*. They had gone through a very thorough Discovery Process. They had pinpointed areas that were not clear or needed attention. They had contrasted the difference if they did not make some changes and had given a big picture of some alternatives.

The synopsis made it pretty simple: would they want to achieve their Needs, Wants, and Wishes 38% of the time or 89% or 99%? It couldn't be clearer.

Mark then began a short talk about Legacy and estate planning. He went over some basics about trusts, wills and probate. Ken had brought along a copy of their trust, which was updated last year, and the team at LionsGate said they would review it. Ken knew that a will was really a "want" and might have little bearing on where you wanted your estate to pass. Probate and aggressive attorneys could hold up the settlement of an estate for years if this part was not right. Mark mentioned philanthropy and some of the options available to give more if that was in the "wishes" portion of the plan.

Both Ken and Karrie supported a multitude of groups working for a better world, and "leveraging" and the utilization of some specific giving strategies was something they would want to hear much more about. They felt they had been blessed and wanted to pass that along to others less fortunate.

As the meeting wrapped up, Mark asked a simple question, "Between now and our meeting next week, the only question for you is, 'Do you want to move forward with LionsGate as your quarterback?'"

Karrie looked at the clock. Wow! Where had an hour and a half gone? She felt like they had been connected to a fire hose, so much great information. Totally different than the last two meetings they had with other planners. She and Ken had a lot to discuss.

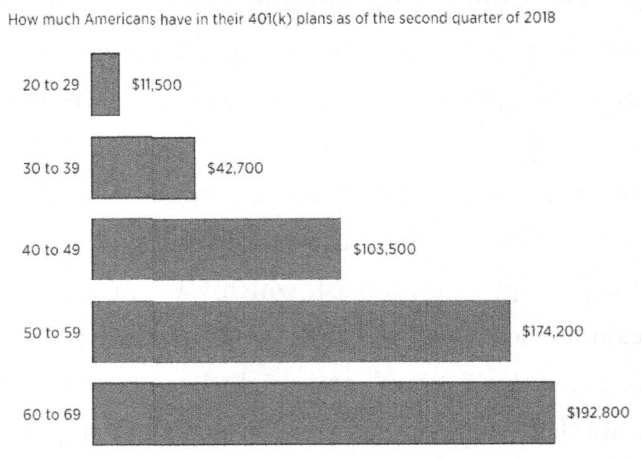

Average 401(k) balance by age

How much Americans have in their 401(k) plans as of the second quarter of 2018

Age	Balance
20 to 29	$11,500
30 to 39	$42,700
40 to 49	$103,500
50 to 59	$174,200
60 to 69	$192,800

CNBC

Americans continue to contribute to their 401(k)s and other deferred taxation plans in record numbers with employer match in many cases. Consistent contributions can even make you a millionaire. In fact, the number of Fidelity 401(k) accounts with a balance of $1 million or more recently hit a record of 168,000, up 41% from last year. (Source: CNBC 2018).

In Chapter 7, we took a hard look at the Theory of Modern Portfolio Management. We investigated its flaws and likened it to how it has been utilized since the advent of the 401(k) in 1981 and the way 95% of financial planners allocated within these plans. This methodology is akin to using surgical instruments from 1950 instead of the modern ones utilized in today's surgical units. This is *not* an appropriate strategy for the distribution of a two-phase of life. Let me say it another way. The old-fashioned pie chart made up of stocks, bonds, and mutual funds has failed repeatedly over the last decade. Monte Carlo-style simulations show that a client using Modern Portfolio Management has a high degree of failure and risks running out of money. It doesn't matter how conservative you think your portfolio is; using an outdated model of financial planning is a recipe for disaster.

Financial planning should be dynamic and changing to fit your current life stage, not a "set it and forget it" one-time plan. Remember: Purpose, Plan, Progress. It will help to steer you successfully through retirement and beyond.

The Lion's Roar:
Key Takeaways from Chapter 9
- Risk tolerance changes as life stage changes. Thus, portfolio strategies should shift as savers become spenders.

- The risks of assets (like stocks and bonds) have increased or decreased risk. This is what you should carefully monitor during your reviews.
- In retirement, it's not so much what you can make as it is what you can spend.

CHAPTER 10

REPLACING THE BOND POSITION

Remember back to a time in your childhood when you first started saving for more than a new bike. Perhaps you, like many, were gifted a bond by your grandparents. "Save this for college," they probably said. *So...this is money?* you probably wondered. Or, fresh out of college, you wanted to do the adult thing and think ahead to retirement, so you socked away a few savings bonds for that hard-to-imagine day way off in the future when your hair had turned gray and your arthritic knees were quacking at you.

Was that the best choice to make at the time? Well...it's complicated.

Interest Rates & Bond Correlation
Some Basics about Bonds

Bonds are a form of debt issued by a company or government that wants to raise some cash. Say Reading Railroad from *Monopoly* fame needs more money to expand their service lines. They would sell bonds that investors like you could buy. In essence by issuing a bond, Reading Railroad is asking the buyers/investors for a loan. So, when you buy a bond, you're lending the bond issuer money. In exchange, the issuer promises to pay back the principal amount to you by a certain date, and sweetens the pot by paying you interest at regular intervals—usually semi-annually.

1. Coupon Interest rate: The coupon rate is simply the amount of interest the issuer will pay to bond holder. If our railroad bond is a 5% coupon on a $100,000 bond, you're going to get $5,000 a year as interest, per year for the life of the bond. At the end of the bond's life, its par value is important to know.

2. Par value: The par value—also known as the face value of the bond—is the amount that is returned to the investor when the bond matures. For example, if a bond is bought at issuance for $1,000, the investor bought the bond at its par value. At the maturity date, the investor will get back the $1,000.

3. Discount Value: Sometimes bonds don't issue at their par values. In fact, they may be issued above or below their par values. Reading Railroad might offer that $100,000 bond to you for $90,000, which is a great deal to you, the buyer. Not only do you get the annual interest payments, at the end of the 10 years, you get not $90,000 back, but $100,000.

4. Premium Value: If a particular bond is issued at a higher value than its par value, it is said to be issued at premium. For example, any bond with face value of $1,000 issued at $1,100 is considered to be at premium. To continue our fictitious railroad device, perhaps their credit rating is exemplary and investors consider this company a sure bet; thus, Reading Railroad bonds are worth more on the trading market than their par value, which means investors must pay more to buy in than the face value of the bond.

Pitfalls of Bond Investing:
- Although bonds are considered safe, there are pitfalls like interest rate risk—one of the primary risks associated with the bond market.
- Reinvestment risk means a bond or future cash flows will need to be reinvested in a security with a lower yield.
- Callable bonds have provisions that allow the bond issuer to purchase the bond back and retire the issue when interest rates fall.
- Default risk occurs when the issuer can't pay the interest or principal in a timely manner or at all.
- Inflation risk: Since bond interest payments are fixed, their value can be eroded by inflation. The longer the term of the bond, the higher the inflation risk. When rates rise, bond prices fall because new bonds are issued that pay higher coupons, making the older, lower-yielding bonds less attractive.

An inverse relationship:
Whenever new bonds are issued, they are generally issued at a coupon rate, which is supposed to be very close to the prevailing market interest rate. Interest rates and bond prices have an inverse relationship, so, when one goes up, the other goes down. ("Why Rising Interest Rates are Bad For Bonds?" *Genesis*, August 26, 2018).

Before the market corrections in 2001-02 and 2007-08, bonds and stocks were correlated. Part of the Modern Portfolio Theory is based upon the premise that when stocks go down, bonds go up. Much to the chagrin of many advisors, in the last two corrections, this maxim did not hold to be true. Equities tanked and bonds lost value due to Market Value Adjustment (MVA).

Bonds were no longer a safety haven.
Although the bond market did not go down as severely as the equities did, there was substantial reduction in value. Not to mention that when investors had to sell, there were genuine losses. In fact, those who were in the "safe" portfolios called "Target Date Funds" (*Fidelity Freedom® 2010 Fund - FFFCX*) experienced some pretty dramatic losses. A Target Date Fund is designed to be a compilation of mutual funds and bonds. Depending on your age, the balance of the fund shifts from the mutual funds to more bonds. The closer one gets to the target date (retirement date, typically around 65 years old), the more the fund shifts to bonds for protection of the principal. Here's the problem with these highly touted "safe retirement funds" in which I see so many pre-retirees invested. The history just doesn't prove out the claims. See below:

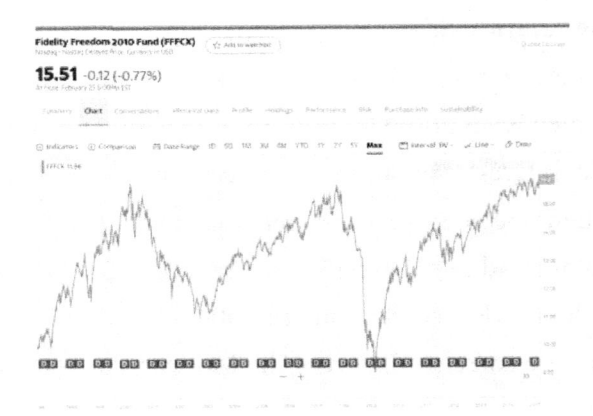

If you were planning to retire in 2008, you began to get pretty nervous on October 8th, 2007 when the fund hit its high point of $15.97 until just 16 months later. Two months after your January 2009 retirement date, on March 2, 2009, it bottomed out at $8.99, a sixteen-month loss of 57%! Does this sound like a good retirement strategy?

Let me repeat: the system is broken.
We are being "sold" products with no real correlation to what is in our best interest. It's wrong and not necessary. It is a sales process driven by the greed of the broker-dealers and the corporate entities they support first over your best interest.

Prevailing wisdom now says that there's no longer a connection between bonds and stocks. **The correlation is now between bonds and interest rates.** Think about it as a seesaw. Remember those from your schoolyard days? If you were the skinny kid and the bigger kid was on the other side, and you were up in the air and he jumped off his end, you hit the ground pretty quick and hard. It's a lesson you did not soon forget.

Well, the same thing can be said for the new correlation of bonds to interest rates. When interest rates go up, bond prices (yields) go down. During the recession of 2008 through 2014, the Fed began pumping money into the economy with quantitative easing (QE). Typically, QE works by simultaneously injecting liquidity and pulling down interest rates. This, in turn, stimulates borrowing and spending activity, which, in turn, promotes economic growth.

When interest rates fall, bond prices rise....

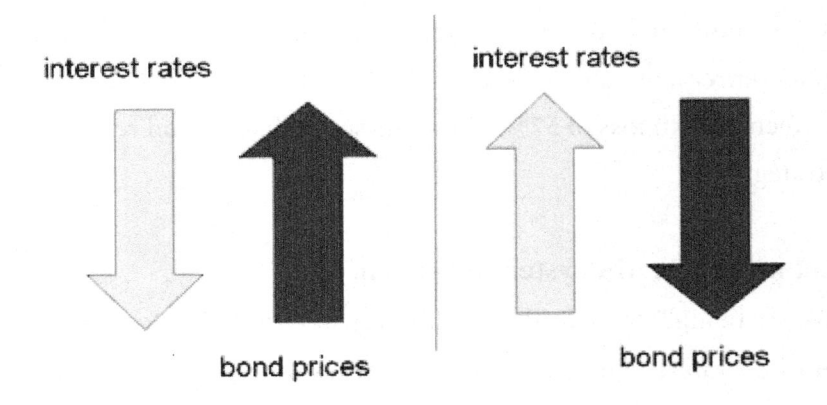

When interest rates rise, bond prices fall....

Fast forward to 2020, interest rates remain at an all-time low. With the new reports since the pandemic, the GDP for Q-2 DECREASED an astounding 32.9%, the worst in decades. In fact, this was the fastest drop in modern record-keeping. Meanwhile, stocks are at all-time highs and interest rates at all-time lows. Bonds are in the tank. Remember, the correlation between bonds and interest rates, when interest rates go down, bonds go up. There is no room for interest rates to go down. So, if they do start going up again (likely), bonds, which already have low yields (returns), have no course to increase their yields.

Meaning, yield (return) on bonds is low. Interest rates have only one way to go: up. And, if IR go up, bonds go down. MVA (market value adjustment) can mean losses in a bond portfolio that in the past would not have been even considered.

US Federal Funds Rate
Effective, Monthly, %

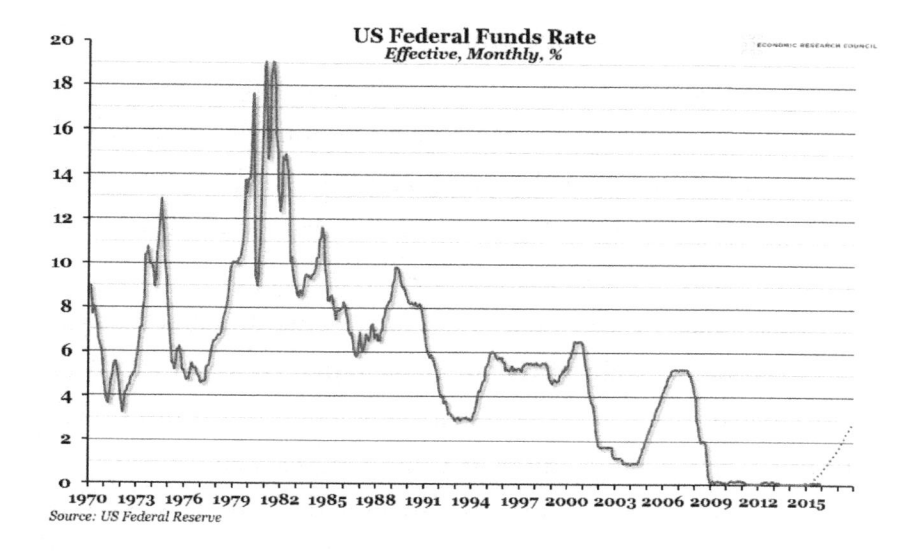

Source: US Federal Reserve

So, where can one park money that replaces the bond position?

Replacing the Bond position in your Portfolio with an Annuity

Before we delve into the specifics of which kind of annuity to utilize when replacing bonds in your portfolio, let's do a quick primer on annuities.

How to Leverage the Strengths of Life Insurance Companies to Replace Bonds with an Annuity

Risk Pooling

Have you ever been to a construction site? Like a site where they are building a large apartment or hotel complex? Have you seen all the safety signs? Some say, "325 Days without an accident." They all work for safety first. That's what a successful retirement plan should embrace. Safety first!

Your Estimated Life Expectancy

When we think about how long we might live after retirement, we can think about our family history: how long did parents and grandparents live? Is there longevity in our family history? How's our physical condition? Do we exercise regularly? How's our diet?

Professors at the University of Pennsylvania developed a system of estimating longevity that was featured in *Time*, the *Wall Street Journal*, and *U.S. News* called "How Long Will I Live?" According to these experts, the average male 65 years old who weighs 187 pounds, is six feet tall, exercises three to four times a week and is in very good health, will have a life expectancy of 90 years.

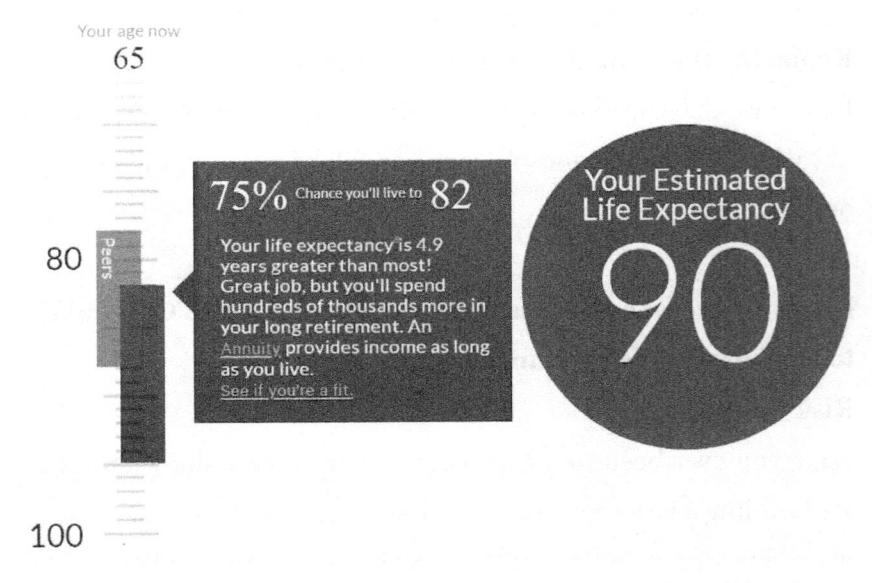

Your age now
65

80

75% Chance you'll live to **82**

Your life expectancy is 4.9 years greater than most! Great job, but you'll spend hundreds of thousands more in your long retirement. An Annuity provides income as long as you live.
See if you're a fit.

Your Estimated Life Expectancy
90

100

Source: https://www.blueprintincome.com/tools/life-expectancy-calculator-how-long-will-i-live/

If you are a female it will be a little bit longer.

(https://www.blueprintincome.com/tools/life-expectancy-calculator-how-long-will-i-live/ to find yours). So, there's a 75% chance that you will make it to 82 and your life expectancy is 90. If you are 65, that's 25 years' worth of savings you will need. And if you are healthy and engaged, you won't just be sitting on the front steps for the last 20 years of your life. You will be travelling, visiting grands, and in general having a pretty good time.

So, you need to play the long game. A retirement income plan should be based on planning to live, not planning to die. Remember the movie *The Shawshank Redemption*? Perhaps the best way to sum up the key to life is wisdom from the movie when Andy Dufresne said to his fellow inmate Red, "Life comes down to a simple choice: you're either busy living or busy dying."

It isn't just a quote from a movie, it's advice for all of us.

We at LionsGate create long-term strategies for our client families. We design strategies that enhance retirement efficiency by simultaneously allowing for more lifetime spending and a greater legacy value for assets.

It's not how much you can make, but how much you can spend. In retirement, income matters. It requires a mind-shift away from accumulation to safety and distribution. (How much can I spend?) Traditional financial planning will almost always fall short or be difficult at best to predict. We must move from the idea that either investments or insurance alone will meet our needs. We need to create a strategy that places an emphasis on insurance products, and how they may behave as part of an integrated retirement income plan. Simply stated, we need our income to last, no matter how long we might live.

How Does Risk Pooling Work?
The first recorded instances of risk pooling (insurance policies) were written over 5,000 years ago to protect shippers against the loss of their cargo and crews at sea. Any one of them would be devastated by the loss of a ship. But by pooling their resources, these ancient businessmen were able to spread the risks more evenly among their numbers, so each paid a relatively small amount. Under the Babylonians, those receiving a loan to fund a shipment would pay an additional amount in exchange for a rider cancelling the loan if a shipment should be lost at sea.

Modern Insurance Policies
The insurance industry grew enormously, as individuals and businesses sought to protect themselves from economic catastrophe by transferring their risks to an insurance pool. We still have commercial shipping insurance—just as we did in the ancient world—and we also insure against such diverse risks as fires, floods, theft, auto accidents, kidnap and ransom schemes, defaults on the part of our debtors, lawsuits and judgments, dying too early, and even against the risk of living too long.

Risk and Premium
A class of professional experts in finance and probability, called actuaries, work for insurance companies to attempt to predict the probability and severity of risk. They also take lapse rates and

interest rates or other expected rates of return on investment into account, with the goal of setting acceptable premiums.

The premium is the cost of pooling one's own risk with that of others via an insurance company and includes the insured's share of expected claims costs, administrative expenses, sales and marketing expenses, and a profit for the insurer. If a premium payer is affected by a covered risk, the insurance company, and not the insured, takes the hit

("What Is Risk Pooling in Insurance?" ZACKS Research - *By: Leslie McClintock | Reviewed by: Ashley Donohoe, MBA | Updated January 28, 2019)*.

Volatility Buffer

The markets are up, the markets are down. Bull run, Bear run, sequence of returns. It's all confusing. What we emphasize for our clients, from the just-retired with a reasonable savings to the ultra-affluent, is to have a volatility buffer. A volatility buffer is just that: in periods of market downturns (and they will happen probably at least a couple of times during your 30-year retirement), these are non-correlated funds that you can turn to instead of taking income from an account that is down in value. It's really pretty simple, but very few people actually get it or practice it.

Consider "Integrating Whole Life Insurance into a Retirement Income Plan: Emphasis on Cash Value as a Volatility Buffer Asset," by Wade D. Pfau, PhD, CFA, and Michael Finke, PhD, CFP. The report considers several asset scenarios of people preparing for retirement. In each case, scenarios including cash value of life insurance policies result in more income for retirees down the road than scenarios that don't include whole life insurance.

"This report shows that using insurance with other investments can really lay the foundation for better outcomes in retirement," said Pfau, professor of retirement income at The American College of Financial Services in Bryn Mawr, Pennsylvania. "We often hear that we don't need life insurance in retirement because we have investments, but this research shows it's harder for the market to beat a strategy with both life insurance and investments."

An advantage of life insurance as part of a retirement strategy is that it provides guarantees that market-based investments can't, said the report's co-author.

"I prefer to incorporate life insurance cash value into an overall investment portfolio as part of a retiree's bond allocation," said Finke, dean and chief academic officer at The American College of Financial Services. "One important advantage of cash value over a traditional bond mutual fund portfolio is the protection against a decline in value if interest rates rise."

Let me give you an example. In the recent past, life insurance has been sold as a protective measure for the death benefit. Especially when younger, one would be sure to have enough life insurance to cover the mortgage on the home, the college for the children and supplemental income for the surviving spouse or partner. The older and more financially secure we became, the less the death benefit was needed. Our house was most likely paid for and the kids were done with college. There were IRAs to create income, pensions and Social Security to secure a known income in retirement and likely no debt. The need for life insurance seemingly was over.

Well, in this new world, we need to go back a couple of generations and look at the way our grandparents and their parents utilized permanent life insurance as an asset class and as a retirement supplement for income.

We often recommend to a 60- to 65-year-old a guaranteed FIUL (Fixed Index Universal Life Insurance) or a whole life insurance policy to create a separate and non-correlated asset class in their portfolio. The benefits of these plans are typically used extensively by the affluent. We sometimes call it the "rich man's Roth." It is a powerful way to build a tax-efficient fund, without the risks of the stock market and one in which the cash value growth of the policy will normally average about 5-6%. We can utilize the cash value as a volatile buffer. So, when the market-based assets are down, we don't have to withdraw. We can withdraw from the cash value of the policy as a loan which is tax free. In a well-constructed life policy, we can create tax-free income for the family when and if taxes go up. This is powerful.

Annuities – Creating Your Own Private Pension Fund
When in Rome do as the Romans do.

Annuities are extraordinarily popular in modern times, but they're not new. In fact, annuities can actually trace their origins back to Roman times.

Contracts during the Emperors' time were known as *annua*, or "annual stipends" in Latin. Back then, Roman citizens would make a one-time payment to the *annua*, in exchange for lifetime payments made once a year.

At LionsGate Advisors, we utilize a very special kind of annuity, a fixed-index annuity (FIA), that is sometimes called a hybrid. It is safe, has predictable growth, and can produce an income stream for life.

All annuities are not alike. In the world of financial planning, there are basically four types of annuities.

The Basics of Annuities

1. The type of annuity

    a. SPIA – **Single Premium Immediate Annuity** – These are safe annuities with guaranteed payments that begin as soon as, or shortly after, you sign the contract and make the single premium. They offer a guaranteed yearly payment with a low interest rate of return. They are generally utilized for Medicaid planning , as they are exempt from spend down requirements.

    b. Fixed annuity – A safe and guaranteed solution that can produce a period of certain or lifetime income. It has a low interest rate (1-3%) and the principle will never be reduced unless you take income from it.

    c. Variable annuity – A Mutual Fund with a life insurance wrapper. It may have riders which guarantee a death benefit or an income stream. It is subject to market swings and has high fees (3-5% or higher). It has sub-accounts which are typically in Mutual Funds and can be managed well or not so well.

    d. Fixed Index Annuity - When you're looking for upside potential with downside protection, a fixed indexed annuity is a tax-deferred, long-term savings option that provides principal protection in a down market and opportunity for growth. It gives you more growth potential than a fixed annuity, along with less risk and less potential return than a variable annuity.

Returns are based on the performance of an underlying index, such as the S&P 500® Composite Stock Price Index, a collection of 500 stocks intended to provide an opportunity for diversification and represent a broad segment of the market. While the benchmark index does follow the market, as an investor, your money is never directly exposed to the stock market.

Under a *deferred* annuity, your money is invested for a period of time until you are ready to begin taking withdrawals, typically in retirement. During the deferral period, earnings are retained which lead to higher payments later. When the owner elects to begin receiving benefits, the deferred annuity is converted into an immediate annuity.

With an *immediate* annuity, you begin to receive payments soon after you make your initial investment.

One of the many answers I get in my classes when we discuss annuities comes when I ask for a show of hands as to who likes annuities or who doesn't. Usually it's about a 70-30 split, those who don't like them lining up as the majority. The trouble is, they don't always have the complete picture. When we drill down on why, they often have misconceptions or misinformation from the internet or one of the large investment houses (as a well-known personality has created an industry slamming annuities and playing on people's fears and greed).

I will ask the question, "If what you thought you knew to be true turned out not to be, when would you want to know?"

Everyone answers the same way, "Now!"

Last year I attended the Rolling Stones concert in Seattle. As I walked from my hotel in downtown to the stadium where the Stones were to perform, I was deluged by large signs and people giving out brochures. Usually these are for local bars or eateries, but these were different. They were sponsored by something called **The Alliance for Lifetime Income.**

The Alliance for Lifetime Income is a nonprofit consumer education organization whose mission is to help Americans understand the need for protected lifetime income from an annuity when planning for retirement, so they don't outlive their money. When I got inside the stadium, I was amazed; the signs were everywhere, promoting websites and giving out information. AT THE ROLLING STONES.

Watching Mick strut across the stage (newly recovered from heart surgery), I realized the pop icons of my youth had indeed aged. Even though they were all over the stage, dancing and singing, from my fifth-row seat, I could see that there were wrinkles and sags that hadn't always been there. Now the sponsor made sense.

Here are a couple of takeaways from the white paper I discovered at The Stones concert:

"Devine & Associates and Milliman, on behalf of the Alliance for Lifetime Income, examined how a significant equity market correction – defined as a 20% market drop within an individual's first ten years of retirement – impacts the risk of running out of income during his or her remaining lifetime."

The analysis suggests that even a family who utilized a fairly conservative 60/40 blend of equities to bonds, and only takes a 4% withdrawal, is at risk. There's a good chance they'll run out of money before they run out of life. Further, if the market corrects early in retirement as opposed to later in retirement, the danger compounds. This is called a sequence of returns risk. None of us know when markets will go up or down; however, whether they happen early in retirement or later can really make a tremendous difference on the availability of funds.

The white paper continues with this shocking survey result:

"…a 2019 survey conducted by the Alliance for Lifetime Income revealed that only 42% of non-retired Americans believe their savings and income from other sources will last their lifetime."

For most families, having a predictable dependable income really reduces the stress in retirement due to the volatility of the markets. Families looking for the predictable dependable income are turning to a solution that protects their investment, produces a predictable return, and income for life. **In other words, money that never runs out. No matter how long you live.**

Index Annuities, An Easy Choice

For many sophisticated investors and families, annuities are an easy choice.

You might say to yourself: "Let's see, I will most likely get a 3-5% return (historically) with the insurance company taking all the risks (see Risk Pooling) I can replace the risky and underperforming bond positions in my portfolio with a no-fee or low-fee (FIA fees range from 0-1.25% approximately), risk-free, guaranteed position. Well, that's a hard choice.

"If I choose, I can 'turn on' the provision giving me a true income for life, even if the principal and growth are depleted. In most cases this will be a percentage of the accumulated value, example: annuity balance of $1,000,000 would yield approximately 5-6% or $50-60,000 a year. And, some of these FIAs have provisions that when the indices increase any year, my income increases. So, an increasing income on a decreasing asset. That's not rocket science.

"And, it can be taken as a joint income or a survivor annuity. So, if it were my IRA and the income rider had begun, if I died, it would continue for my spouse, no matter how long she lived." Your beneficiary will continue to receive payouts for the rest of his or her life after you die. This is a popular option for married couples.

Tax Treatment – The funds you transferred from your IRA (we would rarely recommend a source for funding of this asset except from an IRA) to this account grow tax-deferred. When you take income, it will be taxed as ordinary income (this is why we only use IRA or Roth money to fund these positions).

Lock – Every year or two years, depending on the annuity, the life insurance company locks in the gain on the contract anniversary date (never a loss—the worst a FIA can do is 0%. And in that case, the indices have had a negative year). If the index you and your advisor choose is down, you simply get zero. In this case, with the rest of your equity positions in freefall, *zero* will be our *hero*.

Index Lock – Some annuities allow you can also lock in the gain anytime during the year. With index lock, the owner of the annuity can lock in the index values anytime during the contract year (crediting period), minimizing the effects of midyear market volatility.

Death Benefit – Whatever I don't use for income or withdrawals during my lifetime will pass to my beneficiaries without probate.

Some of these annuity hybrids have evolved to include extended care protection. What I mean by this is, if I (we) are taking income from the lifetime income provisions of the contract, and I have a need for some kind of extended care (home health care, assisted living, nursing home, etc.) the insurance company will *double* my yearly income until the account is depleted, and then, the yearly income will continue at the single rate as before no matter how long I live. It sounds too good to be true, yet it IS true.

Why Annuities Have a Lot of Bad Press
In the recent past, before the 2007-09 corrections, annuities were utilized by broker/dealers extensively. Families trusted the concept and embraced them as people had done since the Roman Empire. Something changed.

In the corrections (recessions) of the early 2000s, annuities (here we are talking about variable annuities, sold by broker-dealers with high annual fees often approaching 4-6%) lost money in their accumulation value.

Broker-dealers sell products that may not be in your best interest. Many large investment firms put pressure on their broker-dealers to sell clients products which have high fees. Companies keep adding additional fees and surrender costs to contracts. Some companies have early surrender charges as high as 20%. Often the fees and charges are hidden in the fine print. Clients feel betrayed by the broker-dealer. In a down market, it's nearly impossible for these annuities to grow, much less maintain their original value. These hidden fees are charged annually and often the only party making money from the variable annuity is the broker-dealer.

A fixed index annuity has fees that range from 0-1.25%. Before you invest, check the insurer's credit rating, a grade given by credit bureaus such as A.M. Best, Standard & Poor's, and Moody's, that expresses the company's financial health. Each rating firm has its own grading scale. As a general rule, limit your options to insurers that receive either an A+ from A.M. Best, or AA- or better from Moody's and S&P. You can find the ratings online or get them from your insurance agent.

While a variable annuity has no guarantees and is subject to market adjustments, a fixed index annuity is guaranteed several ways. The insurance commissioner in each state is a member of NAIC (National Association of Insurance Commissioners). The insurance commissioner regulates companies that do insurance business in that state. Each company must prove on a regular basis that their solvency ratio (the amount of cash reserve they have for each insurer) is a 1:1 ratio. In other words, they must have one dollar on hand for every dollar insured. If they fall below that ratio they must recapitalize or be forced to no longer operate in that state. Their assets and liabilities will be divided proportionally among all of the other insurance companies in that state.

Additionally, there are state guarantee funds that protect annuity owners if an insurance company fails. However, the coverage varies from state to state.

In summation, the correct annuity can enhance your portfolio as a part of a non-correlated strategy.

Why the Right Annuity?
- Income for Life
- Extended Care
- Low Fees
- Guarantees – No market losses
- Risk sharing with an insurance company
- Deferred Taxation
- Replace Bond Position

The Lion's Roar:
Key Takeaways from Chapter 10
- Bonds may not be the safe investment strategy they have been sold to be.
- We are suggesting that some clients replace the bonds in their portfolios with annuities.
- Let the insurance companies take the risk—risk-pooling is very favorable to you!

CHAPTER 11

TAX-FREE INVESTMENTS IN YOUR PORTFOLIO

Tax-Free Investments in Your Portfolio

In the IRS codes, there are only three places we see the words "tax-exempt" and "tax-free." Your Uncle Sam is pretty clear that he does not really want to promote anything that would have these very attractive qualities. The three investment vehicles for this kind of treatment from the IRS are:

- MUNIs – Municipal Bonds
- IRA Roth
- IRS Code 7702 – Life Insurance

In the first part of this book, we discussed the coming tax train, the unfunded liabilities (estimated at this writing to be about $128 trillion and growing by the second), and the heaping national debt (estimated at this writing to be $23 trillion). We also explored the possibility of a sovereign debt crisis and the very real possibility of tax increases for everyone reading these words.

If they happen—tax increases that is—would you rather have a large portion of your retirement in tax-exempt and tax-free income positions? And even if they don't happen, would you still feel better having a large part of your retirement savings coming to you tax free?

Let's take a look at each of these and see how they might fit into your retirement plans.

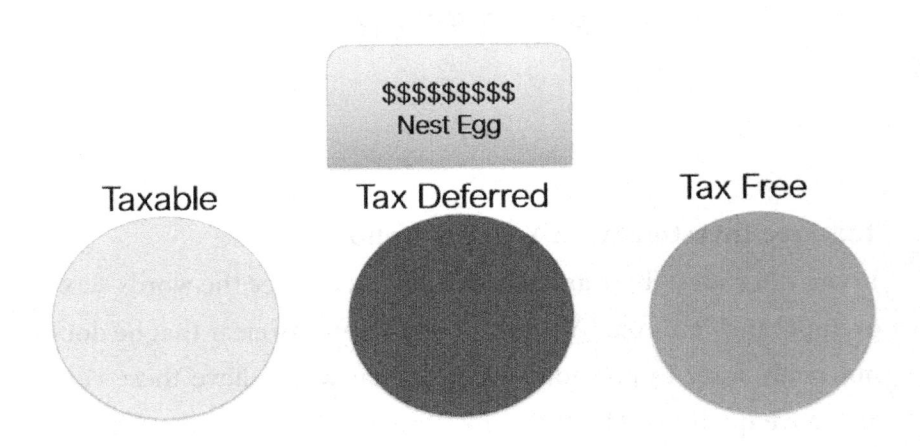

Taxable $$$$$$$$$ Nest Egg   **Tax Deferred**   **Tax Free**

MUNIs or Municipal Bonds
Municipal Bonds are one of the *big three* that have tax-favored characteristics. Having said that, they aren't, as of this writing, the best idea. Interest rates on AAA Rated Muni Bonds are low and on bonds that are not rated as high, the yield will be higher but the risk associated may be prohibitive. Example: would you want to have a large portion of Puerto Rican or Illinois bonds in your retirement portfolio? Puerto Rican bonds defaulted and Illinois bonds are in danger of default at this time.

Municipal Bonds are counted as securities. They are loans that investors make to local governments. They are issued by cities, states, counties, or other local governments for big-ticket items like new schools and roads. For that reason, the interest they pay on the bonds is tax free. In 2018, the municipal bond market was $3.8 trillion.

Advantages

1. Free from Federal Taxes – If you are in a high tax bracket or are seeking to create a tax-exempt income stream for retirement, municipal bonds might be just the thing to supplement your traditional pension, Roth IRA, or 401(k) investments. This tax refuge offers liquidity and tax efficiency all in one, a godsend to those in the highest tax brackets.

2. Free from State and Local Taxes – Municipal bonds are not only exempt from federal taxes, but investments in local municipal development projects are exempted from state and local taxes.

3. Lower Volatility Than Stocks (Fixed Income Assets) – Municipal bonds historically have been one of the safest places to park your savings (short of a savings account or Treasury bonds), while also providing tax-exempt returns and a generally much better return on invested capital than either FDIC-insured accounts or Treasuries.

4. High Level of Liquidity – Municipal bonds are highly liquid and are traded on a secondary market. This means that if you are strapped for cash or need an influx of money for an investment opportunity or emergency, the capital can be accessed quickly and without incurring a tax penalty. This is especially true for investors who invest via ETFs or mutual funds.

Disadvantages

1. Bond Yields May Not Beat Inflation - Municipal bonds are often a conservative investment and they also offer tax advantages, so their yields tend to be relatively low. This means the money you have parked in a bond fund could be worth less in buying power a few years from now than it is today, due to inflation risks.

2. Interest Rate Risk – In this current environment, an investor might be fortunate to find interest rates on AAA rated bonds hovering between 1-2%. Junk bonds and riskier corporate bonds can have greater yields of 4-6%, but are not necessarily worth the added risk. Bonds are supposed to be safe harbors and to have these kinds of high-risk bonds in your portfolio defeats the idea of a safe asset. When interest rates go up, current bonds lose value. This is because bonds that carry a lower interest rate must be sold at a discount to equal current bond yields. This is less of a concern if you plan to hold the bonds to maturity, but it can still be a difficult pill to swallow if you have to cash out bonds or bond funds when they are trading at less than face value.

3. Risk of Default and Loss of Capital – Any investment carries risk. Municipal bonds are no different. Although historically, it's been rare, there's always the chance the municipality could go belly up, in which case your interest payments and principal would be lost.

Bottom line with Municipal Bonds, we like the tax treatment, we are not so excited in this interest rate environment about the return, and we are still a bit shaky on the fundamental foundation of the governments in some cases that issue these. How'd you like to be sitting on $500k of Puerto Rican Bonds?

IRA Roth or 401(k) Roth
One of the very few investments that carry the distinction of growing tax-exempt and tax-free income when used, is the IRA Roth. We advocate a Roth position in your portfolio wholeheartedly. Established by the Taxpayer Relief Act of 1997, the first Roth IRAs were opened in 1998. Named for the legislation's sponsor, the late Sen. William V. Roth Jr. of Delaware, this new type of IRA, funded with after-tax dollars, is intended to help Americans save for retirement while *not decreasing government revenue.*

According to the Investment Company Institute (ICI), contributions were $8.6 billion in 1998 with another $39.3 billion converted from traditional IRAs. By the end of 2019, Roth IRA assets totaled $810 billion.

In 2006, designated Roth contributions were allowed in workplace 401(k) and 403(b) plans, and in governmental 457 plans in 2010. Also, in 2010, all investors—not just those with income less than $100,000—became eligible to convert traditional IRA assets to a Roth IRA.

So, with a Roth, I can pay the taxes when I move funds there, and then it grows without being taxed and comes out tax free when needed. There are no requirements (yet) for RMD (Required Minimum Distribution). Although there are rules on the amount of earned income I can have and still contribute to a Roth, I can "Roth" over any or all of my traditional IRA at once or in stages.

The SECURE Act of 2019 made the distributions to my beneficiaries (non-spousal) problematic. If I inherit a Roth, I must take it all out by year ten. I can let it grow for nine years (tax-exempt) but the new law forces it to all be withdrawn by the tenth year.

If you are still working (earned income), if you file taxes as a single person, your Modified Adjusted Gross Income (MAGI) must be under $137,000 for the tax year 2019 and under $139,000 for the tax year 2020 to contribute to a Roth IRA; and if you're married and filing jointly, your MAGI must be under $203,000 for the tax year 2019 and $206,000 for the tax year 2020.

Because the Trump tax cuts (Tax Cut and Job Act of 2017) expire for income tax and most estate taxes in 2025 (but are permanent for corporations), it is an advantageous time for many to look at a Roth conversion. It's just math. In our practice, we couple these Roth conversions with Federal Tax Credits, which in some cases, eliminate most of the tax expense to move an IRA to an IRA Roth.

7702 Accounts
Life Insurance – The Rich Man's Roth

We love the tax treatment of Roth and though it has some limitations, it still is a great place to have some of your assets. However, there are groups of people who, due to their income, may need to find a different solution.

I remember my first encounter with a life insurance salesperson. I was in my thirties and had been a pretty free spirit in my early years. I had helped to start a yacht brokerage when I was 25, sold Jimmy Buffet his first sailboat (and did some sailing with him, that's another story for another book!), and had great success in these early years. I thought I was invincible both financially and health-wise. I ate all organic and really felt bulletproof. By the time I was 35, I had come to realize how the stars had lined up just perfectly for me in my early years, and those successes were not easy to duplicate later.

I was now the director of a wonderful art gallery in Aspen, Colorado and now had two children, 10 and 12 years old. I was working two jobs to make it and that's when I met the life insurance salesperson. I had gone through a divorce and had gained sole custody of the two boys.

The owner of the gallery decided that my having life insurance would make a lot of sense and she arranged for her agent to visit me. The care and extended feeding of two adolescents was weighing heavy on my mind, and I was more than a little bit anxious about making sure that if something happened to me, the two boys would be taken care of.

His spiel was good as he went through the questions, "How much do you make?" "How much do you have saved?" "How will you care for these two boys if you are no longer on the planet?" "What are your financial obligations," and a few other questions about my annual salary, mortgage calculations, etc.

He used some formulas like, "Your term cover should be twelve to fifteen times your dependent family's annual expenses," and another thumb-rule which says the death benefit should be at least 8-10 times your annual income.

I nodded my head, lost in the numbers, and signed on the dotted line, got a physical, and in a month, was the proud owner of a 20-year term policy for $500,000. Now, it would all be OK if I died.

I had no idea and was pretty clueless. Then 12 years ago, a friend gave me the book, *Bank on Yourself - The Life-Changing Secret to Protecting Your Financial Future* by Pamela Yellen. He was a financial planner, not just an insurance salesman. I looked at the book and thought, "This is the last thing in the world I want to do, sell insurance. Gag me with a spoon!"

I decided to read a chapter just to humor my friend. I began at eight o'clock one evening and sat up until three reading it in one sitting. Wow! This was different. This was really interesting. This was cool. The author asked a very simple question, "If you could be the bank or a customer of the bank, which would you choose?" Of course, I'd be the bank! After all, they have the highest building in just about every city in the country.

And, that's where I began my education on using a properly constructed permanent life insurance policy as an asset class. And wow, it changed my life and those of so many of the families I now serve.

Utilizing permanent life insurance as an asset class requires most of us to undergo a paradigm shift. What is a paradigm shift? It's a perceptual transformation—a change from one way of thinking to another. Einstein said, "The significant problems we face cannot be solved at the same level of thinking we were at when we created them."

We are in new financial territory in 2020. COVID-19 will make—has made—us rethink the way we not only look at our lives and the sudden changes a simple virus has forced us to make for our survival, but also the economic reality of this new world.

The changes we see are akin to the paradigm shift we experienced after 9/11. Our parents and grandparents experienced something similar after the bombing of Pearl Harbor. We will never look at the world in quite the same way.

No one can predict what the course of the markets will be over the next several months or years. While we hope for the best, *hope* is not a strategy. LionsGate Advisors is built upon these pillars: **Excellence, Empowerment** and **Relentless Execution**. Your financial strategy in these times should be built much the same way.

Hope is not a strategy.
Great bull runs like we have experienced the last 11 years make us quickly forget the market volatility of the previous 20 years. Understandably so. The 10 to 20% returns on 401(k) accounts for the last 11 years lulled us into a sense of false security. Very few people, outside of those who study pandemics for a living, could have imagined the swiftness of the spread and the economic impact that was felt almost immediately. At this writing, a large part of the world population is working from home in "shelter from home" orders or suggestions. Unemployment filings are hard to compare to any previous period except to the Great Depression numbers. We are in a new world; no one knows how long it might last or the long- and short-term ramifications to the economy and our very lives.

Again, we can hope for the best, but why not plan for any eventuality?

A properly constructed, over-funded permanent life insurance policy can be an important part of your truly diversified, non-correlated asset strategy. We have been utilizing this tactic for our families for many years. Note that I said it should be a "properly constructed" policy that is a part of a true financial plan. Then, as we have outlined several times already in this book, we need to utilize the following three ideas to make it an important part of your retirement plan.

- **Purpose** – these structures (policies) are not for death benefit alone. They have great benefits for individual or family estate planning and are powerful tactics for business owners to expand, for favorable tax treatments, and for succession. When we recommend that a portion of your assets be in permanent insurance, we have to define the purpose of that asset (just like any other asset).

- **Plan** – As we shift from the accumulation strategies that got us where we are, we need to make sure this asset class is part of our retirement plan. The face of this properly designed asset class can be as different as we each are in looks. A written plan that utilizes this asset class as a volatility buffer can be powerful. Who wants to take withdrawals from an asset that is down? The plan has to be carefully drawn up, leveraging current assets to make the overall plan much better.

- **Progress** – It's not enough to have the right insurance policy in place. Companies and environments change. A properly constructed policy must be monitored closely and at least yearly to expose strengths and weaknesses, with well-thought-out changes as needed. Most life insurance salespeople are done with you after the policy delivery; they may stay in touch to make sure you pay your premiums, but beyond that, they pretty much just let the policy be. This is the wrong course. We must make sure the internal costs of the policies are monitored as well as their allocations and performance.

During the classes I teach for adult learners and with the families we work with at LionsGate Advisors, we want to make sure each retirement design has these four tenets in every plan:

- Applied Knowledge
- Control
- Growth & Income
- Empowerment

Knowledge is why you find yourself reading this book or maybe attending one of my in-person courses. You can also find my remote courses available online. It's another paradigm shift at work! I firmly believe in high education and low tension. Go to our website, www.lionsgateadvisors.com, to the Events section and then Adult Education. The classes are short, 17 minutes or so each, and cover everything from annuities, to life insurance, to extended care, to taxes and the deficit. And, I have just added LionsGate Advisors University as an option. There, you can take the many courses I teach at the colleges and universities at your pace, utilizing a webinar format from the comfort and safety of your home. There are also on-demand classes you can take on your own schedule. Applied knowledge is power!

> *"Wisdom is not a product of schooling but of the lifelong attempt to acquire it." -Albert Einstein*

When I first begin the section of life insurance as an asset class, I can see the looks (during in-person classes) and almost feel the vibe. "Life insurance is expensive, it's front-end loaded, it has large commissions for the salesperson; it is great if I'm young and want to make sure my spouse and children are cared for if I die tragically, but at my age? The returns are low, and I can make so much more in the markets. I don't care about the death benefit; I'm leaving my kids enough. I'm too old."

It's time for that paradigm shift.

In a well-designed retirement plan, one should look at this as a non-correlated, important part of an effective tax and potential income strategy. In the first chapters, we discussed the looming tax crisis in our country. Our economy was already overvalued and on the edge when we began the first round of quantitative easing (printing money) for COVID-19 relief, and bailouts may have to be repeated. The result, as we discussed, is larger and larger budget deficits and no real path ahead. We talked about it being a simple four-letter word, MATH.

> *The revenue to run this expanding government and social system will have to come from somewhere, and the 7702 account is a way to ensure you are not the bank they are robbing.*

Tax benefits aside, these accounts are flexible! Here's why:
- One can self-finance real estate or other purchases or investments by "borrowing" from the policy cash value. You determine the terms of the loan repayment which is collateralized against the death benefit. With a properly constructed policy, one would never have to pay back the "loans" and at death the benefit would be adjusted to pay back the outstanding loans.
- If one does not need the RMD (Required Minimum Distribution) from one's deferred taxation plans, the RMD could be utilized to pay the premium on the life policy, thus placing those disbursements into a tax-exempt and tax-free at withdrawal account and avoid double taxation.
- Over-funding these policies can be very beneficial for tax favorability, because we know over a period of time (75-year lookback) these policies have produced 5-6% returns. They are safe and predictable, especially as a place to have funds in volatile times.

The use of the 7702 Account, permanent life insurance, is a powerful non-correlated asset class that should be in everyone's portfolio. It will reduce your risk exposure and give you the potential for a portion of your income to be tax free.

For more detailed information on life insurance, see my partner, Jonathan Krueger's White Paper in the appendix, entitled: "Funding Life Insurance as a Contingent Asset Class in a Balanced Portfolio."

The Lion's Roar:

Key Takeaways from Chapter 11

- Tax-free investment options include: municipal bonds, Roth accounts, and 7702 accounts (life insurance).
- Plan for an increase in taxes; hope is not a strategy.
- Utilize the "Rich Man's Roth" and teach your kids and grands how it works. This can be the greatest gift you give to the next generation.

CHAPTER 12

HOW TO UTILIZE THE MARKET IN YOUR RETIREMENT PORTFOLIO INCOME IS WHAT MATTERS...

"The pessimist complains about the wind; the optimist expects it to change; the realist adjusts the sails." -William Arthur Ward

When I was a young man, I lived in Aspen, Colorado. It was an incredible spot to be healthy. It seemed like *everyone* was involved in some kind of athletic activity daily. In the summer I would rise early, either plan for a hike to Maroon Bells or go up Independence Pass. I might plan to go for a long walk down the Roaring Fork River, or maybe up Castle Creek to explore and hike. Maybe I'd go for a mountain bike ride up Smuggler Mountain or on the many trails that Snowmass offered. Every day was exciting, the people beautiful and healthy, all with the same mindset of activity.

Nighttime was different. It is expensive to live in Aspen. If you're not a trust-fund baby, you've got to figure a way to support yourself and you need a pretty good income if you want to live in town and not down valley. Many of us worked at least two jobs and one of those was usually in the hospitality sector. My friends and I were the bartenders and wait staff, the hotel maids and desk clerks. I chose to be a bartender and waiter as it afforded me the best opportunity to supplement my day job with maximum income. In 1975, if one could make $100-150 a night waiting tables, that was good money!

There was one catch—it was essentially a commission job. There were a number of factors that could affect my income on any given night. Was I scheduled for a weeknight or a weekend? What was my section? What season was it? Summer or winter? Mud season (spring) or the time before the ski lifts opened the weekend of Thanksgiving? Who was in town? The variables go on and on.

Bottom line, I was on commission. If all the factors stacked up well, I might have a $200 night; if not, I might be sent home early with a small tip jar or maybe even nothing at all. It was hard to plan. That's why I had a day job. It was dependable income, year in and year out. I knew I would at least have that check every two weeks.

If I had a good week, I could go out to dinner or drink at one of the many local bars. I could buy that new bike or snowboard. If the weeks were not so good, I might have to really work to get by.

My philosophy in retirement is modeled in much the same way. Except now that I'm at an age where I'm paying off my second boat instead of my second car, the question becomes not how much I can make, but how much can I spend? I don't want my retirement income to be on "commission," at the whim of volatile times. I want an income I can count on so I can make my plans for travel and more, based upon a steady income that will be affected little by market or economic conditions.

In retirement, I want to follow the 4Ms:

- *Maximizing* **Current Cash Flow,** especially in the early years of retirement
- *Maintaining* your current standard of living
- *Minimizing* cash flow risk
- *Minimizing* short-and long-term principal erosion

These are critical in making sure I focus on what I can spend and don't get distracted by what I can make.

Warren Buffet's mentor, Benjamin Graham, is reported to have said, "The essence of investment management is the management of risk, not the management of returns."

For a commission-free retirement, I believe in the 4Ms. We want to make sure in retirement, it's not how much I can make, but how much can I spend.

Maximizing Current Cash Flow

In early retirement years, I want to make sure I can do all the things I waited 40 years to do while working. I want to travel, visit kids and grands, play golf and not have to worry about cash flow.

Maintaining Current Standard of Living

In the many cases I have designed and then implemented for families now retired, I have rarely seen expenses go down in retirement. In fact, they often increase. Our taxable deductions are reduced: often there is no mortgage and no deduction for that interest, and we are no longer contributing to a deferred taxation plan like a 401(k). Few who I have designed plans for have spent their careers dreaming of sitting on the back porch watching the birds. They are ready to get moving, especially in their early years when they are healthy and can move about easily. That means travel, boats, RVs, second homes; in other words, it means money.

Minimizing Cash Flow Risk

In one of Jimmy Buffet's songs, "We are the People our Parents Warned Us About," he is reminiscing about the good old days and the lyrics are, "Sometimes I wish I was back in my crash-pad days *before I knew what cash flow meant.*" You can never go home!

In retirement, a predictable, steady cash flow is essential to do the things you have always visualized doing after you quit working. If one has to be concerned about the flow of one's cash (essentially one's "paycheck"), it can make for a not-so-fun retirement. It's not just good enough to have assets, one needs to have a dependable allotment of cash to plan and enjoy one's free time. This is what cash flow means.

Cash flow loss in retirement can be catastrophic and certainly discouraging. We utilize non-correlated investments to make sure that in market corrections (like COVID-19), one can gain that all-important cash flow from assets that do not experience such volatility. Not losing is not enough. Having a predictable income is what makes one's retirement less stressful.

Minimizing Short-and Long-term Principal Erosion

To have a solid plan that will meet the hazards of inflation, loss of spouse, long-term care, market volatility and other icebergs of the retirement journey and not sink your ship, focusing on this "M" is vital. The markets are good mitigations against inflation as well as being a part of your legacy planning. If one can prevent principal erosion of this portion of your strategy, it will serve powerfully to achieve those two results.

To produce a consistent income in retirement, I believe in utilizing the power of yield or dividends.

Dividend Definition - Investopedia

www.investopedia.com › Stocks › Dividend Stocks

A dividend is the distribution of a portion of the company's earnings, decided and managed by the company's board of directors, and paid to a class of its shareholders. Dividends are payments made by publicly listed companies as a reward to investors for putting their money into the venture.

All dividend stocks, ETFs, and Mutual Funds are not created equally. In our practice, we manage a portfolio simply called the Known Return. It is managed to have the greatest yield balanced with the prevention of the erosion of principal. It is structured to pay out healthy dividends of 5-6% a year after fees, year in and year out. If the markets correct, the dividends are monitored to produce the same percentage. Remember, dividends are paid on number of shares, not necessarily the value of those shares. When allocations in this portfolio are selected, it is based upon the underlying economic strength of the funds or companies. Sectors can go down, but often the underlying strength of the asset is strong, even though it might correct for stock price values.

Think of it this way. If you owned an apartment building (value of $1.5mm) of 100 units and it had 100% occupancy, you would expect to receive rent checks every month. In "normal" times, with full occupancy (let's say you received $1,000 a month per apartment) you would receive $100,000 a month.

If the real estate market declined and the new value of the apartment building was down 30% and was now worth $1,050,000, you would still receive the same rental checks each month (assuming again 100% occupancy).

If the real estate market values were increasing and the value of your property increased 30%, it would now be worth $1,950,000. Unless you increased the rent, your monthly rental checks combined would still be $100,000.

In the declining real estate market, you would not have a "loss" unless you sold the building. In the appreciating real estate market, you would not have a "gain" unless you sold the building.

In either market, assuming occupancy was consistent, you would rely on that income of $100k a month. It would be known return.

In retirement, with the management of a portfolio of $2mm, producing 5-6% dividends a year, one could reliably expect a $100-120,000 income from the "rental of those apartments."

If the markets are up or down, the strategy is designed to produce these same dividends or yields. This is a buy and hold strategy where the only changes in positions are when an asset in the portfolio is underperforming (dividend yields) or is taking a major hit on its valuation. Sometimes, adjustments are made to the percentages of each position in the portfolio and occasionally a change of positions is indicated.

All of these adjustments are made utilizing a data-centric overview, tracking technical sides of the markets, the economy and the companies or funds within the portfolio.

During the year, my clients monitor the ups or downs of those funds and positions, but look to see what has been either deposited in their bank accounts (dividends and interest) or what has been reinvested if they don't need the income, buying more positions which then can produce more dividends. It works.

As in all of the strategies outlined in this book, recommendations are individual based upon your Risk Tolerance and suitability. Investment as outlined above can be part of a strategy for a family only after many factors have been taken into consideration.

What's the right course for your retirement ship? The most important two words in financial planning: "It depends."

The Lion's Roar:
Key Takeaways from Chapter 12

- Portfolio management in retirement should ensure steady income, so investors should strive always for non-correlated funds.
- It is possible to structure a portfolio to return a steady income each month, regardless of market corrections. At LionsGate, we call that the Known Return plan.
- Make sure your income is not like commission. Make it dependable.

SECTION III

THE THIRD ACT

CHAPTER 13

WHEN TO TAKE SOCIAL SECURITY

Remember when you first asked a customer if they'd like fries with their burger or carefully bagged those cereal boxes separately from the precious tomatoes? Whatever your first job was, you probably labored for two weeks thinking about what you might buy with your hard-earned cash. Then you got that first paycheck and asked, "Wait...who is this FICA guy and why is he taking my money?"

Deciding exactly when you get to reclaim some of that FICA contribution in the form of Social Security can be a real challenge and there are a lot of opinions out there. Everyone's situation is a little bit different. For some of my clients, the best time is right now. For some, it makes a whole lot of sense to wait until age 70.

Let me explain. We always run a "break-even" analysis when we look at a couple who have just retired or are close to retirement. When we go through our Discovery portion of our first meeting, we are asking very specific questions to ascertain information about their **Needs, Wants, and Desires.** We look at sources of income in retirement, expenses in retirement, health care costs, etc. We also want to know how their health is now and how long their parents and grandparents live(d). We want to know if one of the spouses has the potential of a longer life than the other. We want to know how much each spouse contributed to the Social Security Trust Fund and for how many years. Do they have pensions? How large is their IRA and what have they saved outside of retirement accounts? What is the age difference between the spouses?

Then, we work a plan, utilizing a very advanced spreadsheet that takes into consideration taxes now and in the future (we believe taxes will increase), inflation, health care costs, and any inheritances they might receive.

Only then can we, as fiduciaries, recommend the optimal time to take Social Security and whether we utilize Spousal Benefits to increase their payments over a specific time.

I took my Social Security at age 66 because I felt like I could do a better job investing the monthly payment than my Uncle Sam could *and* if I died, I'd have that in a fund that my beneficiaries would receive. Also, in my case after age 66, I could make as much as I wanted without a penalty for taking my benefit. It may seem elementary, but if you postpone taking Social Security and you die, those benefits go away (the exception is that if you are married, the surviving spouse can take the larger of the two benefits—yours or theirs).

Social Security is underrated as an investment annuity. A typical yearly payout of an annuity is 5%. The average Social Security check is $1502.92 per month or $18,035 per year; the largest Social Security benefit in 2020 is $3,011 or a yearly benefit of $36,132. To create this same kind of income with a retirement account, one would have to have $360,480 for the smaller benefit and $722,640 for the larger. Think about it. This is money you can't outlive and has historically had a yearly increase derived from the COLAs (cost of living adjustments). It's a pretty good deal.

We recommend you complete a break-even analysis of your potential benefits before you make a decision on Social Security strategies. A financial breakdown is often not enough. You must take into consideration a multitude of determinants, including:

- your health
- your spouse's health
- how does longevity run in your family?
- which of the spouses has the larger benefit?
- Spouses can claim benefits, where appropriate, on their partner's work record and that could be as early as age 62.
- Will you or your spouse work part time in retirement?

It is vital to take all the factors into consideration before you file for Social Security benefits.

How Benefits Are Calculated

In the world of Social Security vernacular, we determine your Full Retirement Age or FRA using the year of your birth.

Here's how they arrive at your eligibility for Social Security at the present time:

Take a look at the chart on the following page.

Social Security in 2020

Determining your Social Security full retirement age (FRA)

Year of birth	Social Security FRA	Age 62 reduction
1941	age 65 and 8 months	23.33%
1942	age 65 and 10 months	24.17%
1943-1954	age 66	25.00%
1955	age 66 and 2 months	25.83%
1956	age 66 and 4 months	26.67%
1957	age 66 and 6 months	27.50%
1958	age 66 and 8 months	28.33%
1959	age 66 and 10 months	29.17%
1960 and later	age 67	30.00%

If born on January 1, use the prior year of birth. Social Security Administration, Benefit Reduction for Early Retirement

Depending on the year in which you were born, your full retirement age will be between 65 and 67. Unless you are disabled, the earliest age at which you can claim Social Security benefits is 62.

Here's how they calculate the actual benefits for 2020.

Social Security benefits

Maximum monthly benefit	$3,011
Earnings limitations and benefit reduction	Before FRA ($1 for $2 benefit reduction): $18,240/year
	Year up until first of month one turns FRA ($1 for $3 benefit reduction): $48,600/year
	After FRA: no reduction

Social Security Administration, Fact Sheet, 2020.

Social Security benefits taxation (income in retirement causing 0%, up to 50%, or up to 85% of Social Security benefits to be taxable)	Single or HOH up to 50% taxable: $25,000 MAGI up to 85% taxable: $34,000 MAGI Married, filing jointly up to 50% taxable: $32,000 MAGI up to 85% taxable: $44,000 MAGI

Benefits Planner: Income Taxes and Your Social Security Benefits

Let's just make it simple. If you begin your benefit prior to your full retirement age, say at 62, you will essentially have a 25% to 30% permanent reduction compared to a scenario where you had begun those benefits at full retirement age. If you wait to the maximum age of 70 to begin your benefits, you will have an 8% per year compounded growth to that benefit or 132% of your primary insurance amount.

If you wonder whether you may work and still collect your benefit, the answer is yes. You can work *and* collect Social Security at the same time. Here's the challenge. While you are working, the SSA will reduce your benefit by the amounts shown in the chart below until you reach your full retirement age.

Working and Collecting Social Security

Age	Benefit Reduction	Earned Income Limits for 2019
62 Until Full Retirement	Lose $1 for every $2 earned above limit	$17,640
Year of Full Retirement Age	Lose $1 for every $3 earned above limit	$46,920
After Full Retirement Age	No benefit reduction	No limit

Sources: SSA.gov, 2019

When you make that decision of when to take your benefit, it might be helpful to look at the chart below.

When Should I Start Taking Social Security Benefits?

Collecting Social Security Benefits Before and After Full Retirement Age

Change in Benefits vs Age:
- 62: -25%
- 63: -20%
- 64: -13.3%
- 65: -6.7%
- 66: 0%
- 67: 8%
- 68: 16%
- 69: 24%
- 70: 32%

Source: SSA.gov, 2019. Does not include cost-of-living increases.

Assumes Full Retirement Age is 66

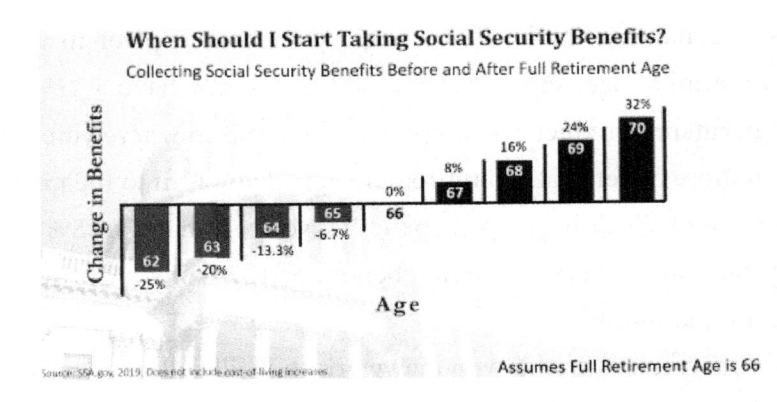

COLA

Your Social Security benefit has had increases many years. It's called a cost of living adjustment, or COLA. It's not something you can count on year after year (see 2001 & 2006) but it has averaged 1.52% over the last 10 years. That is significantly lower than the actual cost of living adjustment. So, your spending power can actually diminish. Here's how COLAs have increased over the last 10 years compared to the cost of living.

Social Security cost-of-living adjustments (COLAs)

Note: Percentage increase to benefits received, starting in January of the year indicated

Year	COLA (%)	Year	Year
2001	3.5%	2011	0.0%
2002	2.6%	2012	3.6%
2003	1.4%	2013	1.7%
2004	2.1%	2014	1.5%
2005	2.7%	2015	1.7%
2006	4.1%	2016	0%
2007	3.3%	2017	0.3%
2008	2.3%	2018	2.0%
2009	5.8%	2019	2.8%
2010	0.0%	2020	1.6%

Social Security Administration, Cost-of-Living Adjustment, 2020

Maximizing Spousal and Survivor Benefits

As we addressed briefly earlier in this chapter, the Spousal and Survivor Benefits are a possibility you must examine prior to deciding when to take either of your Social Security benefits.

If a parent left a career to become the full-time caregiver to children at home, that spouse may not have earned the work credits to qualify for their own Social Security benefit. So, there is a solution for this.

Ken and Karrie are a good example. Even though Karrie had worked for some of her adult life, as a couple, they had made the decision that Karrie would stay at home during the early years as their children grew. She was officially out of the work force, but as we know, it's a full-time job raising children and running a functioning household. So, Karrie stayed home working while Ken worked at an "official" job. Karrie had the forty quarters of work to qualify for a Social Security benefit, it was just much lower than Ken's.

In this case, or in a case where one of the spouses had a much higher income than the other over the years, the spousal benefit option is a good one to consider.

At age 62, Karrie qualified to receive benefits based upon Ken's work record. Under this scenario, the most Karrie can receive is half of Ken's benefit. Since Ken's benefit was around $3,000 a month (for demonstration), Karrie *could* receive a "partial benefit" (see chart below) at age 62. At full retirement age, Karrie could receive up to almost half of Ken's benefit. If Karrie waited to take the spousal benefit until Ken (the primary worker) had applied for SS at full retirement age (66 for Ken), then she would now receive almost half of Ken's. In this example, about $1500/month.

If there was a smaller difference in the benefits that Karrie would receive (if she took half of Ken's) then she could take the half of Ken's, let her own benefits grow at about 8% a year compounded, and switch to her own benefits (if that amount was more than half of Ken's) at age 70. It's a bit confusing, as the government seems so very good at being, but it is worth exploring these options *before* you take either of the benefits.

If you have questions, the best resource is to go to your Social Security office in your hometown and let them help you with the options. They cannot give you advice, so come prepared with the right questions to ask.

Maximizing Spousal and Survivor Benefits

	Collect When	Eligible for Partial Benefit	Eligible for Maximum Benefit
Spousal Benefit	Primary worker is still alive and has applied for Social Security benefits	Spouse is at least 62 and will collect 32% to 49.9% of full benefit	Spouse is at retirement age and will collect 50% of full benefit
Survivor Benefit	Primary worker is no longer living	Survivor is at least 60 and will collect 71.5% to 99% of full benefit	Survivor is at full retirement age and will collect 100% of benefit

Sources: SSA.gov, 2019

Tax Considerations for Social Security Benefits

Another way to maximize your income while reducing taxes is to take as much income as possible from sources that are excluded from your provisional income. Provisional income is the income the SSA uses to calculate the taxation of your Social Security benefit, like your Roth IRA or a nontaxable pension.

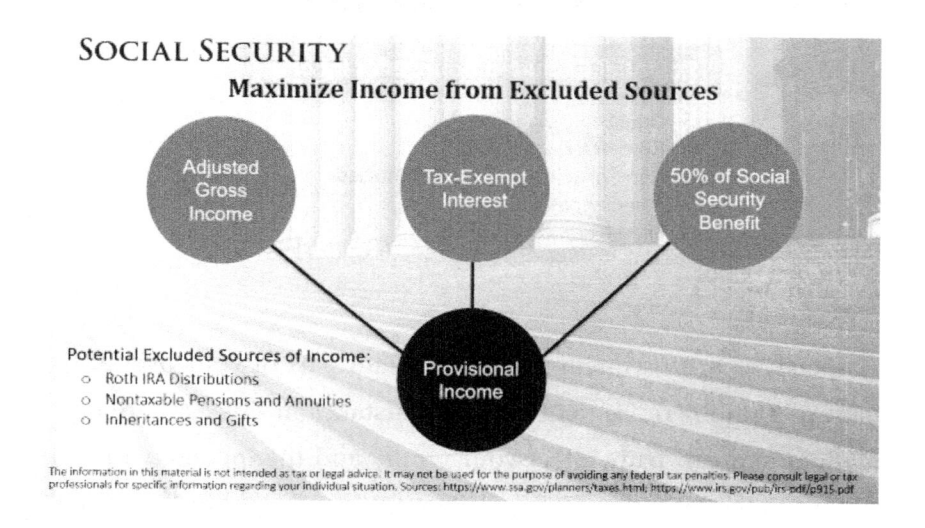

SOCIAL SECURITY
Maximize Income from Excluded Sources

- Adjusted Gross Income
- Tax-Exempt Interest
- 50% of Social Security Benefit

→ Provisional Income

Potential Excluded Sources of Income:
- Roth IRA Distributions
- Nontaxable Pensions and Annuities
- Inheritances and Gifts

The information in this material is not intended as tax or legal advice. It may not be used for the purpose of avoiding any federal tax penalties. Please consult legal or tax professionals for specific information regarding your individual situation. Sources: https://www.ssa.gov/planners/taxes.html; https://www.irs.gov/pub/irs-pdf/p915.pdf

Calculating Provisional Income

Once you've decided when to start drawing your Social Security benefits, you're not done figuring. There are tax implications to consider. Provisional income is an important part of how the taxes on your Social Security are calculated. Provisional income is defined by the IRS as the sum of wages, taxable and nontaxable interest, dividends, pensions, self-employment, and other taxable income, plus half of your annual Social Security benefits.

There are ways to structure your income that can minimize the impact of these taxes. See the chart below. At LionsGate, we help our families to determine how to best plan for the greatest inevitability, taxes.

AGI + Tax Exempt Income + 50% of Social Security Income = Provisional Income

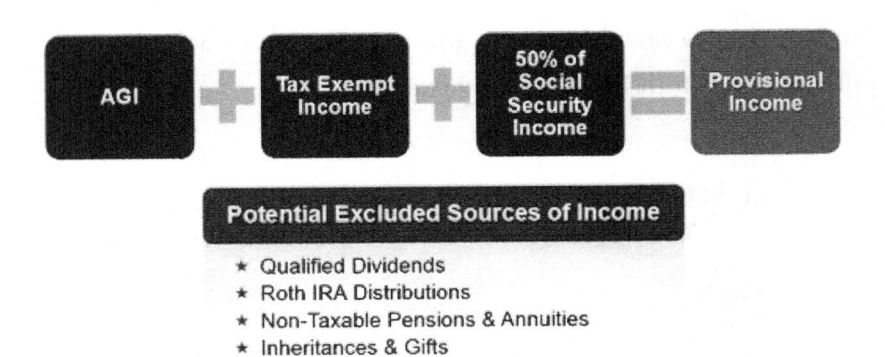

Potential Excluded Sources of Income
- ★ Qualified Dividends
- ★ Roth IRA Distributions
- ★ Non-Taxable Pensions & Annuities
- ★ Inheritances & Gifts
- ★ Life Insurance Proceeds

A Social Security strategy is an important part of your overall financial plan for retirement. Critical mistakes in this area are permanent and can truly affect your family and the income you will receive in the retirement journey. No strategy is right for everyone. Be sure your strategy for SS is aligned and coordinated with the rest of your retirement plan. Factors including age differences between you and your spouse, health issues, and life expectancy can affect your overall outcome.

The details matter.

Some Thoughts on Medicare

Medicare is a foundation of health care for most retirees. Some retirees are fortunate enough to have military health care or even to have their supplemental (Medigap) coverage paid for by their former employer. For most of us, Medicare is the health care insurance we rely on during our retirement.

Medicare Part B - The "hold harmless rule"

If you are currently taking Social Security, there is a special rule that ensures Social Security benefits will not decline from one year to the next because of increases in Medicare Part B premiums. The "rule" was activated in a year in which the Social Security COLA amount was not large enough to cover the full amount of their increased Medicare premium. Below are the current (2020) premiums for Medicare:

Modified adjusted gross income (MAGI) 2018 tax year	2020 held harmless (HH)	2020 not held harmless	Premium level
Individual ≤$87,000 Married, filing jointly ≤$174,000	< $144.60	$144.60	23.33%
Individual >$87,000 up to $109,000 Married, filing jointly >$174,000 up to $218,000		$202.40	24.17%
Individual >$109,000 up to $136,000 Married, filing jointly >$218,000 up to $272,000		$289.20	25.00%
Individual >$136,000 up to $163,000 Married, filing jointly >$272,000 up to $326,000		$376.00	25.83%
Individual >$163,000 up to $500,000 Married, filing jointly >$326,000 up to $750,000		$462.70	26.67%
Individual >$500,000 Married, filing jointly >$750,000		$491.60	27.50%

Centers for Medicare and Medicaid Services, 2020 Medicare Parts A & B Premiums and Deductibles.

Prescription Drug Plan – Part D

Some prescription drug plans have different levels or tiers of co-payments, with different costs for different types of drugs. Average monthly premium, deductible, and/or coinsurance varies by plan. Below are the costs associated with Part D.

Modified adjusted gross income (MAGI) 2018 tax year	PART D 2020 monthly premium
Individual ≤$87,000 Married couple ≤$174,000	Plan premium
Individual >$87,000 up to $109,000 Married couple >$174,000 up to $218,000	$12.20 + plan premium
Individual >$109,000 up to $136,000 Married couple >$218,000 up to $272,000	$31.50 + plan premium
Individual >$136,000 up to $163,000 Married couple >$272,000 up to $326,000	$50.70 + plan premium
Individual >$163,000 up to $500,000 Married couple >$326,000 up to $750,000	$70.00 + plan premium
Individual >$500,000 Married couple >$750,000	$76.40 + plan premium

Medicare.gov, Monthly premium for drug plans, 2020.

The Lion's Roar:
Key Takeaways from Chapter 13

- Not everyone will start receiving Social Security benefits at the same time.
- Be sure your strategy for SS is aligned and coordinated with the rest of your retirement plan. The details matter.
- Know the spousal options and make a decision based upon fact and logic. It's important.

CHAPTER 14

LIVE, QUIT, OR DIE
AN HONEST CONVERSATION ABOUT EXTENDED CARE

"The conversation began for 400,000 people in 1969 on Max Yasgur's farm when Wavy Gravy stood on the stage in Woodstock, NY on Sunday morning to say, 'We've got to feed and take care of each other!' Now, years later, many of those Baby Boomers and their sisters and brothers who have spent their lives having fed and taken care of children and those in need, face a future they could little have imagined; having their children put aside potentially years of their lives to take care of them and the resulting consequences of doing so."

This quote from the book, *The Conversation* (Harley Gordon, Acanthus Publishing, 2018) speaks to the difficulty we all have talking about this eventuality. I highly recommend that you purchase this book, read it, and pass it along to someone you love.

You may be thinking that Extended Care, or what is also called Long-term Care is not your problem. I mean, you've done a great job of taking care of yourself. You go to the gym, play tennis, and swim. You eat pretty healthy and your parents lived into their late eighties. Your spouse's mom is going strong and walks daily. What could possibly go wrong?

Plenty.

It's a known fact that people are living longer. According to the Institute on Aging, there are more than 40 million Americans who are age 65 and older, and that figure is expected to increase as the last of the Baby Boomers reach age 65. Many of my clients and our generation in general are quietly worrying about how we can best prepare for our future health care needs, as well as how to pay for supportive services or senior living accommodations.

Extended care is not only a life-changing event for an individual, it's also life changing for the family. Preparing can help lessen the impact. There are good options that exist.

Extended Care Coming to a Facility Near You

No longer the "old folks' homes" of previous eras, extended care is care that provides the ability to live out the last phase of our lives as *comfortably* and with as much *dignity* as possible.

It may surprise you to know seven out of ten 65-year-olds will need extended care in the future.

It may also surprise you to know 8% of people between 40 and 50 years old have a disability that could require extended care services.

"At a time when many hardly have their retirement fully funded, it pays to look into the options for long-term care and what kind of costs are involved with Long-Term Care Insurance Plan, re-

gardless of your age. Having the facts can save you money long-term, and help you come up with a financial plan to weather difficult times."

By Mila Araujo
Updated February 21, 2017

The truth is that if you are not allocating a portion of your assets for extended care, you are allocating all your funds and risking even more. Extended care is about your future and your family's.

Being unprepared for extended health care can have a big impact, not only on your life, but also that of your spouse and your family. Your spouse may feel an obligation to become the caregiver, or perhaps the financial situation will dictate it. The stress and responsibility of being a primary caregiver can often make the caregiver ill as well.

If a spouse isn't involved, often children or other loved ones carry the burden.

We believe a healthy, stress-free retirement is built around these four keys:

LIONSGATE

4 M's – The Key to Comprehensive Retirement Income

- *Maximizing Current Cash Flow,* especially in the early years of retirement
- *Maintaining your current standard of living*
- *Minimizing cash flow risk*
- *Minimizing short and log-term principal erosion*

Extended health care needs can interrupt your retirement, place an undue burden on your family or spouse and quickly deplete your resources and liquidity. A properly designed plan to address these potential needs will make you sleep better and be prepared IF it becomes an issue.

In each area of a state and the country, extended care costs can be quite different. When we examine the costs in St Louis, this what we find:

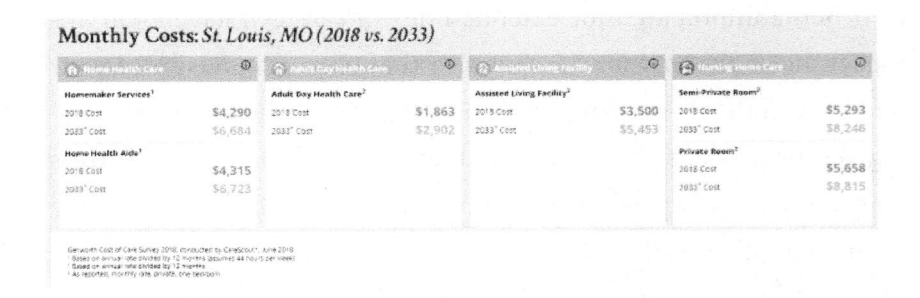

Monthly Costs: *St. Louis, MO (2018 vs. 2033)*

Home Health Care		Adult Day Health Care		Assisted Living Facility		Nursing Home Care	
Homemaker Services[1]		**Adult Day Health Care[2]**		**Assisted Living Facility[2]**		**Semi-Private Room[2]**	
2018 Cost	$4,290	2018 Cost	$1,863	2018 Cost	$3,500	2018 Cost	$5,293
2033* Cost	$6,684	2033* Cost	$2,902	2033* Cost	$5,453	2033* Cost	$8,246
Home Health Aide[1]						**Private Room[2]**	
2018 Cost	$4,315					2018 Cost	$5,658
2033* Cost	$6,723					2033* Cost	$8,815

Genworth Cost of Care Survey 2018, conducted by CareScout®, June 2018
[1] Based on annual rate divided by 12 months (assumes 44 hours per week)
[2] Based on annual rate divided by 12 months
* As reported, monthly rate, private, one bedroom

There are several ways to fund extended health care that we will examine.

- Traditional long-term care insurance
- Government programs
- Self-funding
- Asset-based long-term care strategies

We believe just as you would set aside some of your retirement assets for income, some for a cash reserve, and some for legacy, you should also have a strategy that will insulate the rest of your assets in the event you need expensive extended care.

Let's discus the merits of each.

Traditional long-term care insurance can be a great way to prepare for extended care, if care is needed; the problem is that we have no way of knowing if we are the ones that will be needing care.

Many don't like the idea of another bill to pay and qualifying for coverage can be a challenge. Long-term care insurance also brings the possibility of future premium increases—potentially making an affordable premium unaffordable in the future.

And let's be honest. In the end, there is also a loss of choice and control. All the more reason to leave yourself options by planning ahead. Here's a chart on the typical costs of a Long-Term Care Insurance Policy in St. Louis according to Genworth Insurance Company:

Traditional Extended Care Costs

Policy Type

Is this an individual or couple?   ○ Individual   ● Couple

	Individual 1	Individual 2
Gender	○ Male ● Female	● Male ○ Female
Age	65	67

Coverage

Daily Maximum	$200 Per Day	$200 Per Day
Benefit Multiplier	4 Years	4 Years

Calculate >

Annual Premium Estimate	$3,187.11	$3,993.72

Source: Genworth Insurance Company 2017   For educational purposes and are hypothetical.

Medicare only provides rehabilitative services. It does not pay for long-term care. Medicare covers up to 100 days of skilled nursing care per illness. To qualify, you must enter a Medicare-approved skilled nursing facility or nursing home within 30 days of a hospital stay that lasted at least three days. The care in the nursing home must be for the same condition as the hospital stay.

Medicaid is a government program that does pay for long-term care; however, it is needs-based. Benefits can vary from state to state and you must first spend down your own assets before qualifying. In addition, popular care options like assisted living and home care may not be available. And, this option can mean a loss of choice and control.

Government Programs
- Medicare – only provides rehabilitative services, does not provide long- term
- Medicaid
    - Benefits vary state by state
    - Must 'spend down' your assets first
    - Some options like home care & assisted living may not be available
    - Can mean loss of choice and control

If you haven't prepared for extended care, or do not feel the need to, what you are doing is called self-funding. Simply put, if there is an extended-care need, you will bear the entire cost and risk. Assets can be set aside "just in case." However, the problem is not being able to know how much is enough. Some people can afford to absorb the cost of a few years of care, but what if the need becomes greater? What if care lasts 10 years? Ten years at $10,000 a month, often the cost of a memory unit, we are looking at $120,000 a year! Ten years, $1,200,000.

And, what about the tax treatment? Self-pay does not take advantage of the Pension Protection Act (or PPA). Passed by Congress in 2006, the act went into effect in 2010 and had a significant impact on our annuity products and utilizing them in a tax-advantaged way to pay for extended care. The PPA allows federal tax-free withdrawals for qualifying long-term care events from annuities funded with non-qualified dollars.

Self-Funding
- Bearing the entire risk of an extended care need
- Setting aside assets 'just in case'
    - IRAs, cash, annuities, etc…
    - Some can afford to absorb costs for a few years
    - Taxed as utilized (either as ordinary income or capital gain)

Another option is called asset-based extended-term care. This option consists of specific insurance products based upon life insurance and annuities. Some advantages they offer include income-tax-free care benefits, benefits even if care is never needed, and the ability to obtain premiums that are guaranteed to never increase.

In recent years, clients who purchased traditional extended-care insurance long ago will bring us a new bill from the company that asks them to pick from either higher premiums (we have seen as much as 50%) or reduced benefit ($150/day going to $100/day). Neither of those choices are good ones. The companies that issue these policies cannot raise your rate alone but must go to the insurance commissioner in each state and request an increase across the board, detailing how it is needed to keep the companies' business in this venue solvent. They almost always get the nod. Which leaves consumers in the lurch.

Predictably, we will see these increases happen more and more as the baby boomers age, their lives extended because of medical innovations, and they need more care for more years. It's just that pesky four-letter word again, MATH. The numbers must make sense and math doesn't lie or have grey areas.

Asset-based long-term care benefits
- Specific products based on life insurance and annuities that can provide long-term care benefits
- Some advantages
  - If care is needed, asset-based long-term care products could provide income tax free benefits
  - If care is never needed, asset passes to next generation
  - Some companies offer premiums that are contractually guaranteed never to increase

Using Leverage as a Financial Tool in Your Retirement Plan
There are three good ways to leverage your current assets that you may not be utilizing for income to provide tax-efficient and reliable extended care if needed.

Traditionally, Leverage is an investment strategy of using borrowed money—specifically, the use of various financial instruments or borrowed capital—to increase the potential return of an investment. Here's where it's different when we talk about using leverage in your personal financial plan.

We're not borrowing money from somewhere else, but from ourselves. Yet, we want to accomplish the same results: ***to increase the potential return of an investment***. Let me give you an example. Real estate investors are often highly leveraged in the traditional financial sense; they may purchase many investment properties with low equity and use that equity to buy more. If all goes well, it does. If the real estate markets are in a bubble or if the investor over-leveraged and there is a correction or interest rates go up, the house of cards can collapse (and did in 2008).

We are advocating the use of financial leverage in your retirement plan by *not* increasing (in most cases *decreasing*) the amount of risk in your portfolio. It's a powerful way to make your money work for you in what seems like two ways.

Let me explain.

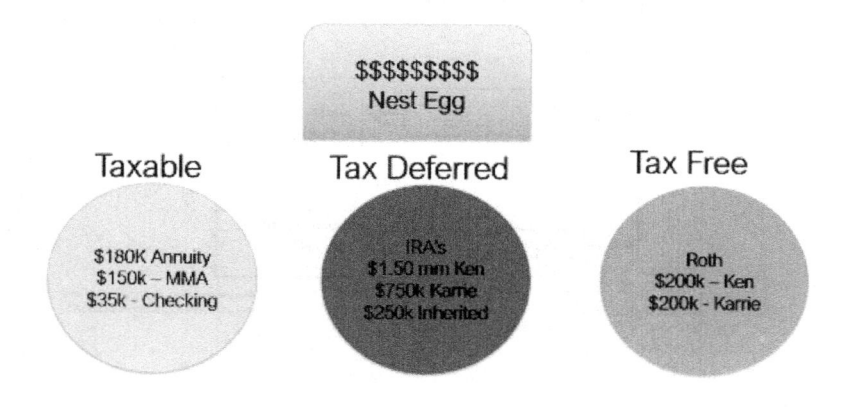

$$$$$$$$
Nest Egg

Taxable
$180K Annuity
$150k – MMA
$35k - Checking

Tax Deferred
IRA's
$1.50 mm Ken
$750k Karrie
$250k Inherited

Tax Free
Roth
$200k – Ken
$200k - Karrie

Most of us who have done well have a large portion in that tax-deferred (postponed) bucket in the middle. We may have become enlightened that this is a "ticking time-bomb" and we may have decided to begin to move it from this place *before* taxes inevitably increase. We may have a strategy to Roth over some of this each year. That's a good idea.

Let's see how to identify a Purpose (addressing the possible need for extended care for both), a Plan (asset-based extended care) and a way to monitor the Progress. In this case, they also became *keenly aware* of their tax time-bomb, their lack of a plan for extended care (Pinpoint), the alternatives to self-insuring (Contrast) and then the cost of that self-insurance for this possibility (Calculate). Now, they must decide whether to make a change. See how the process works?

Here is a hypothetical example (it will be different for each family depending on age, health, etc.). Karrie and Ken decided to rollover $300,000 of Ken's IRA into an Asset-Based Hybrid LTC annuity/Life Insurance strategy.

Life Events

Single Premium: $300,000*

- Live a long life and need long-term care → LTC benefit: $10,253 for 50 months + Optional lifetime LTC benefits $2,676 annual premium
- Decide to quit or surrender the policy → Year 15 surrender value: $347,828
- At death → Death benefit: $512,688

*Based upon joint male and female, both age 65, non-smoker, preferred underwriting class, minimum 4% cash value accumulation, minus cost of insurance.
**Joint life not available in PA.

Source: State Life Insurance Company

Numeric examples are hypothetical and were used for educational purposes only.

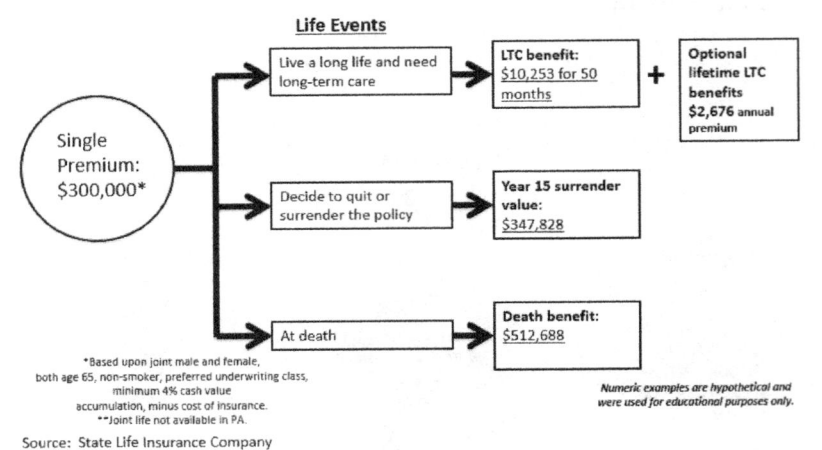

Illustrations featured in this presentation are only for educational purposes and are hypothetical.

The couple transferred, with no taxable event, same as a rollover, $300k from Ken's tax-deferred retirement account (IRA). This single premium will now fund an extended care policy for *both* Ken and Karrie, giving them $10,253 a month each should they need extended care.

Live

Look at the chart again. If an extended care situation arises and either one or both need home health care, assisted living, nursing home, or memory care (among other cares), the monthly benefit shown will kick in for those expenses. In this scenario, between the two of them, they will have that benefit for fifty months, or if both needed the care at the same time, it would last twenty-five months. When that "pot" runs out, the benefits stop. If they chose to pay the additional "Optional Lifetime LTC" of $2,676 a year (this would have to come from a source other than their IRA), their coverage would be Lifetime Unlimited for *both*. Regardless of how long they had to have the benefit, it would be there. Worst-case scenario might be 10 years in a memory unit. An additional yearly fee will provide protection from inflation at 3%.

Sounds too good to be true but let me tell you more. If they died before receiving any of the benefits, the death benefit ($512,688) would go to their beneficiaries, in most cases tax free. Let's say Ken needed the benefits for a year and he received the $10k each month for his care, then died. And, Karrie had the protection in place, but never needed any care and died several years later. In this scenario, the beneficiaries would receive the difference between what Ken used, $123,036, and the death benefit of $512,688, or $389,652. They started with $300k and received—leveraged—it into at least $512k. If it had been 10 years since they made the move to leverage a small part of their IRA to have available for this Purpose, all of the benefits utilized for extended care would be tax free. We like that.

If they had self-insured, the $123k used for Ken's care would be taxed as either ordinary income or a capital gain. What if Ken had needed five years of care? Pinpoint, contrast, calculate—that would be $615,180 or for 10 years, $1,230,360. With this strategy as part of a plan, they now have that benefit tax free and its lifetime.

Quit

Now, look again, the middle portion where it says, "Decide to quit or surrender the policy." This is the quit part of live, quit, or die.

Maybe they received a huge inheritance and decided to move to New Zealand; they could surrender the policy, for *any* reason (remember, this is a very specialized second to die life insurance policy designed specifically for extended care) and receive the greater of the surrender value, or at very minimum, the amount of the single premium paid ($300,000 in this case).

If on the 31st day or any day after the policy goes into force, the full return of premium is provided.

Die

If neither Ken nor Karrie ever need the policy and live long, happy lives, the death benefit would then pass to their beneficiaries, tax free. What if they used some of the benefits, say in year ten, Ken got ill and needed some assistance, and they chose to engage a home health care company to assist Karrie, which cost $5,000 a month. Ken either didn't need it after 10 months or he passed on ($50,000 total of the benefit utilized); then if Karrie lived another five years, the benefits would be available to her at up to $10,253 a month. And, if Karrie then passed, the difference between what was used for Ken's care and the death benefit would pass to the beneficiaries ($512,688-$50,000 = $462,688).

This is the best, by far, of any of the asset-based extended care solutions on the market today. The company that offers this plan has been in business over a hundred years and is rock solid.

Another Twist -1035 Exchange

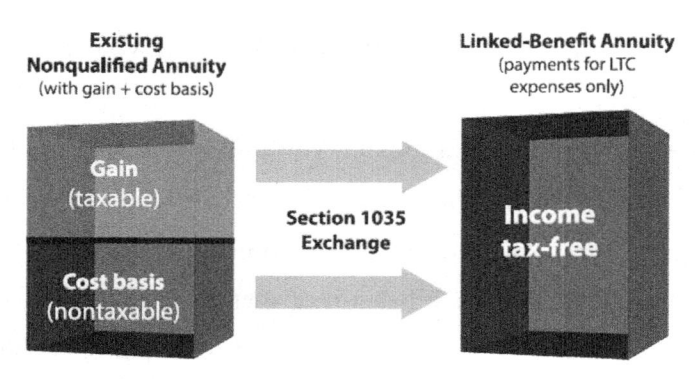

Existing Nonqualified Annuity
(with gain + cost basis)

Gain (taxable)

Cost basis (nontaxable)

Section 1035 Exchange

Linked-Benefit Annuity
(payments for LTC expenses only)

Income tax-free

The American Association for Long-Term Care Insurance, Guide to Long-Term Care Planning Using 1035 Exchanges 2019

The Pension Protection Act (or PPA), passed by Congress in 2006, went into effect in 2010 and had a significant impact on annuities.

The PPA allows federal tax-free withdrawals for qualifying long-term care events from annuities funded with non-qualified dollars.

This allows you to reallocate existing non-qualified annuities with significant taxable gains, which may have already been earmarked for an emergency, to an annuity with LTC benefits and receive tax-free dollars for LTC expenses.

Additionally, our eligible person provision allows you to transfer an annuity with a single owner or annuitant and add your spouse as an eligible person, allowing both of you to access dollars tax-free for LTC.

So, you were smart twenty years ago, knowing you might need some kind of long-term care in the future. When you inherited $75,000 from Great-Uncle Buster, you purchased an annuity that sat and grew, knowing that if you ever needed long-term care you would have that $75k and the growth to use for your care.

Over the last 20 years, it has now grown to $180,000 and you're feeling warm and fuzzy about this decision. The cost basis is $75,000 and the growth $105,000. You'd pay taxes on the $105,000 when used.

But what if you took that annuity, and utilizing PPA, completed a 1035 exchange into PPA-Qualified Linked Benefit Annuity? All of that $180,000 could now be used for LTC tax free!

Comparing Options
Nonqualified Annuities

Let's look at a typical situation to compare the potential benefits of repurposing an existing nonqualified annuity at age 65.

For example, a 65-year-old individual owns a nonqualified annuity obtained at age 49. The cost basis is $75,000 with an average annual return of 2.5% for a traditional annuity and 1.5% for a linked-benefit annuity. Values are projected to age 85, when the likelihood of needing LTC is greatest.

USING YOUR TRADITIONAL ANNUITY
To pay for LTC expenses

Gain = $105,000 Taxable
Cost Basis = $75,000 Nontaxable

Available amount for LTC costs at age 85
$180,000 (projected)
Accumulated value/cash surrender value (age 85)
$180,000 (projected)

Withdrawals to pay for qualifying LTC care
36 months @ $5,000/month (age 85)
$105,000 SUBJECT TO INCOME TAXATION

USING A 1035 EXCHANGE TO REPURPOSE INTO A PPA-Qualified Linked-Benefit Annuity
Annuity is repurposed at age 65, and the 1035 Exchange amount is $110,000.

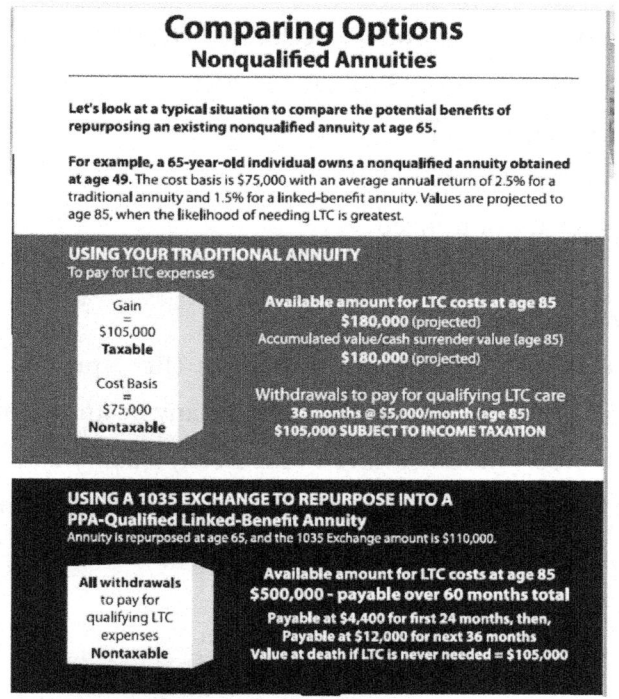

All withdrawals to pay for qualifying LTC expenses Nontaxable

Available amount for LTC costs at age 85
$500,000 - payable over 60 months total
Payable at $4,400 for first 24 months, then,
Payable at $12,000 for next 36 months
Value at death if LTC is never needed = $105,000

The American Association for Long-Term Care Insurance, Guide to Long-Term Care Planning Using 1035 Exchanges 2019

Rider to Life Insurance Policy

Many whole life and universal life insurance policies offer a path to extended care. Riders on these policies simply allow you to accelerate the death benefit for that need. It allows for tax-free distribution (I love the sound of those words) of up to $380 a day for 2020. The IRS changes these amounts regularly, and you are restricted to the formula they use. That daily benefit amounts to about $11,400 a month, enough for the best nursing home in the area.

Chronic Care Rider on Permanent Life Insurance

- Must medically qualify for insurance
- Tax-free distribution – Accelerated Death Benefit (IRS limitations) – up to $380 a day for 2020
- Leverage of asset
- Non-correlated asset
- Legacy if not utilized

Annuity Doubler

Some specialized Fixed Index Annuities (FIA) provide another measure of protection and do not require any heath examinations. In other words, you don't have to medically qualify as you would for **Live, Quit, or Die** or for the life insurance solution discussed above.

Annuity Doubler – Fixed Index Annuity - FIA

- No medical qualifying
- Guarantees or Index Strategies
- Income Doubler for Extended Care Purposes Including Home Health Care
    - Example
    - $500,000 FIA
        - Income $500k x 5% = $25,000
        - Care doubler twice income - $50,000
            - Until exhausted or five years in most cases
            - Then reverts back to the original income

For educational use only.

What are the six basic activities of daily living?

What are the activities of daily living?
- Eating
- Bathing
- Dressing
- Toileting (being able to get on and off the toilet and perform personal hygiene functions)
- Transferring (being able to get in and out of bed or a chair without assistance)
- Maintaining continence (being able to control bladder and bowel functions)

With a properly constructed FIA from the right insurance company, one has the option of taking what is called Lifetime Income, meaning, when you need more income for your plan, you can "switch this on" and begin to receive an income for life based upon the income value of the annuity. For example—and this is just an estimate, it can be a bit different with each company and the ages of the annuitant—if you had a FIA and the income value was $500,000, the yearly income would be around $25,000. If you had an extended-care need, the company would then *double* that income for up to five years ($50,000 a year) or until the cash value of the annuity was depleted. Then, the yearly income you receive would go back to the original $25,000 and continue for the rest of your life, even if the account balance is zero!

How to have THE Conversation
Regardless of the path you choose, it's important to be prepared for extended health care. Remember, it's about your future and your family's. The good news is that options exist and being prepared can help lessen the impact. In the book, *The Conversation*, the author explains that women and men are hardwired very differently when it comes to facing the issue of needing assistance. Here is an excerpt:

"Men believe they have two tasks to perform: find food for the home and to protect those in the home. Their brains are constructed to dismiss the risk of performing these tasks. It's natural, therefore, to dismiss the risk of needing extended care (or of dying or becoming seriously disabled during working years for that matter) because it would undermine their basic directives. In fact, if you are a male and you believe your role is to provide for and protect others, do you think there is any chance of these events happening to you? No…

Women view the issue of risk very differently. Although they also believe, as do men, that they will not need care (or die or become seriously disabled during working years), they are predisposed to take a more nuanced approach to the subject...

Men generally believe there are no *ifs, ands,* or *buts* of needing care. Women, when asked if they believe they will need care, will often hesitate and then answer...*they hope they don't need care.*"

Having the extended-care conversation with a loved one can be difficult and this little book made it so much easier for me and many of my clients.

At LionsGate Advisors, we believe that extended-care needs can take the best plan for retirement and put it into failure. If you self-insured, why would you want to have such a large investment that might go to caring for you or your family? You did not get to where you are today by making bad decisions. You are aware of taxes and how to mitigate them successfully. It's the smart move to seek an advisor to help you find the best long-term care strategy in much the same way.

The Lion's Roar:
Key Takeaways from Chapter 15

- Because of better health care, most of us are going to end up needing long-term care in our elderly years, which means, most of us are going to need to save for that expense in one way or another.
- If you are not allocating a portion of your assets for extended care you are allocating all your funds and risking even more.

- For some, the best strategy to fund elder care is to use tax-free investment funds to purchase an Asset-Based Hybrid LTC annuity/Life Insurance strategy.
- Do you want to live with the kids? Do they want to live with you? Then, do nothing.

CHAPTER 15

THE FAMILY OFFICE

"If we command our wealth, we shall be rich and free. If our wealth commands us, we are poor indeed." -Edmund Burke

A person's own family is, without a doubt, the greatest wealth that person will ever possess. How to successfully pass this sentiment from one generation to the next can be a real challenge.

Shirtsleeves to shirtsleeves in three generations is an American translation of a Lancashire proverb, "There's nobbut three generations atween a clog and clog."

In a recent article appearing in *Forbes* (January 28, 2019), author Dennis Jaffe outlines this well.

"The 'shirtsleeves' curse refers to the very real danger of declining family wealth across generations. Hearing it triggers fear in family leaders, for it not only asserts that family fortunes dissipate over generations, but also that the cause of failure lies with their heirs. It implies that the second and third generations of a family are lazy and unmotivated and use up the fruits of their elders' hard work. And by demeaning the younger generations, it suggests that wealth creators have the higher virtue and must use their wisdom to set up such structures as conditional trusts to 'take care' of their less capable and less noble heirs."

The term Family Office may be something you are familiar with, but most likely not. If your family's wealth is north of $100 million, you may know of and participate in this type of organization regularly. If you are affluent but not to the tune of $100 million, this might be a new term that you are not sure of and how it works.

At LionsGate Advisors, we have seen the need for this kind of management of a family's wealth begin at a much lower number, $5 million and up.

In an online book, *The Single-Family Office* by Richard Wilson, which has been downloaded over 83,000 times globally, this structure is explained well.

"A family office is 360 degree financial and wealth management firm and personal CFO for the ultra-affluent, often providing investment, charitable giving, budgeting, insurance, taxation, and multi-generational guidance to an individual or family. The most direct way of understanding the purpose of a family office is to think of a very robust and comprehensive wealth management solution which looks at every financial aspect of an ultra-wealthy person's or family's life."

Most wealth management firms are not specialists in tax mitigation, charitable giving and utilizing very specialized life insurance policies as an asset class and how to work with a multi-generational plan. Having a team that can coordinate these functions and your trusted advisors is how LionsGate Advisors works in the Family Office space.

When the first generation (Gen1) makes the money, the next generation (Gen2) may have directly witnessed the parents as they built their wealth. Dinner conversation may have included reports on the growth of the family business, or even how to buy the cars and the next larger home (cash, finance, etc.).

As Gen1 ages and looks to successfully pass the wealth they have accumulated to Gen2 and Gen3, they want to have a plan built that can be followed and to make sure that Gen3 and Gen4 don't have to reinvent the wheel.

Often by Gen3, there is little to link the work Gen1 did to their day-to-day lives. Gen1 made sacrifices and often have a strong desire to make sure their successors don't have to work like they did.

So, how do we have the conversation about family wealth? How do we set up a plan to make sure Gen2 and Gen3 understand how to pass their wealth to the next generation?

Working with a Family Office instead of a single CPA, estate attorney or traditional wealth management firm can make a huge difference.

- More control and direction of where every dollar is spent in managing your wealth holistically.
- Central financial management for the wealth so more holistic decision making can be done.
- Higher chance of an efficient and successful transfer of family assets, heritage, values, and relationships.

- Access to institutional quality talent, fund managers, and resources that would be difficult or impossible to obtain as an individual.
- Reduced costs in achieving a full balance-sheet financial management and investment solution.

Establishing a Family Office will help you as you implement a *Family Compass*. You will begin with Mission, Values, and Goals. This mission statement, like that of any good company, will establish the groundwork for your goals, values, and vision.

Finding the right financial team to steer this process is critical as is knowing your mission, values, and goals. Once you determine those for your Family Office, you can seek out the planner with the same orientation.

Next, you will create a system of *Governance Policies*. This is how you will communicate as a family, how decisions will be made on how to invest, how to give and how to distribute to the family. This will act as the guide.

Regular meetings are a key essential in the success of your Family Office, and should be conducted as a retreat with expenses paid from a common pot of money set aside for this yearly or more frequent meeting. A great Family Office will be stronger and get better as communication is prioritized.

The Lion's Roar:
Key Takeaways from Chapter 15

- For ultra-affluent families, outsourcing the wealth management services to one firm can preserve the wealth and ensure that decisions are made in a holistic manner.

- Educating your children and their children is the key to making sure the assets you pass to each generation will be powerful in their lives. This is one of the greatest gifts you can give to your children and grands.

CHAPTER 16

SECURE ESTATE AND LEGACY PLANNING

As I begin this chapter, let me first tell you that I am not an attorney and cannot give you legal advice. The content of this chapter is to *steer* you in the right direction. Only a licensed attorney can offer advice and draw up any of the documents mentioned in this chapter.

The most successful and creative retirement plan will not go beyond the first generation if the estate and trust planning is not tuned in with the issues in the economy, including taxation. Most of us have wills and we normally have a DPOA (Durable Power of Attorney), Living Will, and Advanced Healthcare Directive. This is the bare minimum, although for some estates this is all that may be needed.

Estate Taxes
Most of us will not have an estate tax issue if we die today. The current estate tax exemption for an individual is about $11.58mm or for a couple, almost $23mm. In today's environment, this is only an issue for the ultra-affluent.

However.

If we're reading the tea leaves correctly, there may be some changes on the horizon. We believe that when the estate tax changes made in the Tax & Jobs Act of 2017 expire in 2026, there is a very real possibility that Congress will lower those exemptions. In the not-so-distant past, estate tax exemptions have been as low as $120,000 (1977) and have escalated slowly to today's $11.5mm.

Federal Estate Tax Exemptions 1997 Through 2020

Year	Estate Tax Exemption	Top Estate Tax Rate
1997	$600,000	55%
1998	$625,000	55%
1999	$650,000	55%
2000	$675,000	55%
2001	$675,000	55%
2002	$1,000,000	50%
2003	$1,000,000	49%
2004	$1,500,000	48%
2005	$1,500,000	47%
2006	$2,000,000	46%
2007	$2,000,000	45%
2020 - $11.58mm		

———

When the Estate Tax Exemption expires in 2026, regardless of who is in office, we must prepare for a change.

———

So, even if your expected estate is $3-5mm, it might make sense to have a proper trust and tax mitigation in place.

Estate planning should be done at the bare minimum because:
- It's your right
- Avoid probate
- Minimize taxes
- Make health care decisions
- Plan for incapacity

A trust is a fiduciary arrangement that allows a third party, or trustee, to hold assets on behalf of a beneficiary or beneficiaries.

Trusts

Trusts can be arranged in many ways and can specify exactly how and when the assets pass to the beneficiaries. Since trusts usually avoid probate, your beneficiaries may gain access to these assets more quickly than they might to assets that are transferred using a will. Additionally, if it is an irrevocable trust, it may not be considered part of the taxable estate, so fewer taxes may be due upon your death.

Bottom line, a trust can save your heirs time and court fees, and potentially reduce estate taxes as well.

A deep dive into this area of estate planning could take up a whole book. There are many types of trusts, including Testamen- tary, irrevocable life insurance trust (ILIT), Charitable Remainder trust

(CRT), Generation-skipping trust (GST), and more. Again, the best advice here is to have a basic understanding of trusts and how they work; then have your trusted advisors work together to create the best situation for you and your family.

When we "quarterback" the family retirement plan, we do just that; we coordinate the efforts of each of these trusted advisors to make sure they all know the plan and are onboard with the projected outcome. Remember: Purpose, Plan, Progress.

When we meet with families, we always ask to see their trust. Many do not have one and for those who do, sometimes it has not been updated in many years. Laws change, and this important document is one you need to review every few years or anytime there is some fundamental change in your situation or a life-changing event.

Just as we discussed in the section about extended care, talking about trusts can also be sticky conversations. Just like needing more care than we can get at home, confronting the prospect of our deaths can be uncomfortable, for both parents and adult children. We all want privacy and even with family members that can be an issue.

In estate planning, there can be very significant financial and personal benefits in having your trustee and potential survivors aware of your intentions after your death. Begin a dialogue with those who will have to carry out your wishes and instructions so they are comfortable with what you want. Have them understand what you want done in the event that you are incapacitated. While initiating the conversation can be daunting, doing so allows your family to take advantage of some of the best tax strategies. Facilitate these discussions in a period of relative calm and not in a crisis.

Types of Family Trusts

Revocable trust: Also known as a living trust, a revocable trust can help assets pass outside of probate yet allow you to retain control of the assets during your (the grantor's) lifetime. It is flexible and can be dissolved at any time, should your circumstances or intentions change. A revocable trust typically becomes irrevocable upon the death of the grantor.

You can name yourself trustee (or co-trustee) and retain ownership and control over the trust, its terms and assets during your lifetime, but make provisions for a successor trustee to manage them in the event of your incapacity or death.

Although a revocable trust may help avoid probate, it is usually still subject to estate taxes. It also means that during your lifetime, it is treated like any other asset you own.

Irrevocable trust: An irrevocable trust typically transfers your assets out of your (the grantor's) estate and potentially out of the reach of estate taxes and probate, but cannot be altered by the grantor after it has been executed. Therefore, once you establish the trust, you will lose control over the assets and you cannot change any terms or decide to dissolve the trust.

An irrevocable trust is generally preferred over a revocable trust if your primary aim is to reduce the amount subject to estate taxes by effectively removing the trust assets from your estate. Also, since the assets have been transferred to the trust, you are relieved of the tax liability on the income generated by the trust assets (although distributions will typically have income tax consequences). It may also be protected in the event of a legal judgment against you.

Financial planning should be able to change as your life and the circumstances change.

Probate & Special Circumstances

I am not an attorney and the information below is not legal advice. You should contact an estate attorney to see what provisions you might need in your estate plan.

As above, when we go through the Discovery part of our review with a new family or business, one of the most important questions we ask is, "Do you have a revocable trust?" And, "When was it last reviewed?"

In our litigious society, more and more often the *wishes* spelled out in a will are not the end result in the settlement of the estate. You may think your estate is too small to worry about a trust, but you might be wrong.

We all hear about celebrities who pass without a will or trust, and can't believe it. The latest one was Aretha Franklin, the Queen of Soul. Others who have died in recent years include Prince, Michael Jackson, Amy Winehouse, Bob Marley, Jimi Hendrix, Sonny Bono, and Kurt Cobain. All of them passed without leaving clear instructions for their successors.

A properly constructed living or revocable trust can keep things out of probate and make them private. Probate is the legal process that takes place after someone dies. It ensures that property and your possessions are passed on to the people you intend. It makes sure your taxes and debts are paid correctly. Finally, it validates a will (if you have one) and makes sure the directions in that will are carried through.

If your estate is simple and you have only a home and personal possessions, a trust may not be necessary. Often TOD or Transfer on Death will suffice to make sure those possessions pass to your beneficiaries. A word of caution here: it is not always a good idea to have one or more of your beneficiaries as "joint" on your bank accounts or other personal assets. As a joint owner, if they had a lawsuit filed against them, it is possible that your "joint" property could be attached and you dragged into the suit.

If you have a child with special needs, a trust set up for those situations may be essential. The purpose of a special needs trust is to provide for a person with disabilities without jeopardizing government benefits. Most estate attorneys will recommend this type of trust be set up before a child turns 18. This trust will provide stability and security for a family member should something happen to the creators of the trust. This trust will be held for the benefit of the child and will offer the maximum flexibility.

Again, reach out to an attorney who works in this venue to make sure your child and you are protected.

If you are a blended family, a trust may be important to ensure that when one of you dies, the biological children from each previous marriage (and any children you had together) receive their "fair" portion of the estate.

Even in a situation where you and your spouse have been together a long time, it is important (and a revocable trust can establish this) that your assets pass to the children and grandchildren and not necessarily the spouse of your child. Sometimes, marriages don't work out and the last thing you want is for the ex of your child to end up with a piece of your estate.

Within a properly constructed trust, one will usually find Financial Powers of Attorney, a Pour-Over Will, Advanced Healthcare Directives, and Living Wills. Do your homework on this and make sure it is complete. A good revocable trust will cost you typically around $2,500-3,500. This is a great investment.

The Lion's Roar:
Key Takeaways from Chapter 16

- We expect estate taxes to change in the coming years, which may make it necessary for even moderately successful professionals to establish a trust and tax mitigation plans.
- At a minimum, all familiespeople should have an attorney advise them whether they would benefit from a trust and which type draft a willwould to ensure that theiryour estate isn't trapped in probate after your passing.

CHAPTER 17

IT DEPENDS

Perhaps the two most utilized words in financial planning are "It depends." And, how true it is! We are all complex beings and our thoughts and needs are just as complex. As the saying goes, one man's trash is another man's treasure.

Over the years I have had the great pleasure of assisting many families on their retirement journey. In Chapter One, I likened it to sailing across the Atlantic Ocean on a small sailing vessel. I think that analogy holds true and is more and more relevant as the new "normal" of a pandemic and the consequences both socially and economically set in, and we try to make adjustments in our lives.

Change is the Only Constant
As I write this, it's the end of a three-day weekend during which my wife and I worked around the "ranch," installing some four-board fencing to keep our wonderful dog, Romeo, from the road. He is 10 and in the past few weeks as we have shifted to sheltering in place and working from home, Romeo has a new behavior that he never exhibited in the past. One of our neighbors walks his three large dogs on our gravel road in the country several times a day (he is a professor and is teaching remotely this semester). The

dogs are great explorers and have taken to coming onto our land for a quick look around. Well, that drives Romeo crazy. His new normal is to take off after those intruding beasts and make sure the area is safe for Mommy and Daddy.

He's a good boy. But he's a small dog and we worry about the occasional traffic we get on our road. Sometimes folks have a tendency to drive a little too fast and may be looking at their cell phone or in deep thought about the day ahead. Romeo tends to dart into the road and, like a bunny or squirrel, he might not be seen until it is too late.

We are worried sick.

So, we began the arduous task of building a fence with two gates as a way to at least delay his path, keep the other dogs out, and hopefully save Romeo from disaster.

Normally, on a four- or five-day weekend, we would jet off to St. Martin or even for a quick trip to Sicily for some great food and a sail on our boat. It's not happening this year or for the foreseeable future. So, for love of our dog, we are building a fence. Our circumstances have changed and we must adapt, just like in the world of financial planning. The bonus is that it's helping us to stay fit!

Reading the Warning Signs

In a September 2020 report from the nonpartisan Congressional Budget Office, it was noted, "For the first time since World War II, the U.S. government's debt will roughly equal the size of the entire American economy by the end of this year… The CBO reports the debt will amount to 98% of the nation's gross domestic product. Last year it was 79%."

What has changed? The spending due to COVID-19.

In the first part of this book, I likened the runaway budget deficit to Wile E. Coyote and the story where he sees the train coming down the tracks on course to hit his shed (pulled onto the tracks by the Road Runner), and he simply pulls the shade down.

Our collective heads are buried in the sand. The deficit, which has been running at an unsustainable $1 trillion+ a year for the last 12 years, is now projected by the CBO to be over $3.3 trillion by the end of this fiscal year.

G. William Hoagland, a senior vice president of the Bipartisan Policy Center and former Republican staff director for the Senate Budget Committee, said, "It will be hard to ratchet down this spending going forward, and we are going to be entering a long stretch of deficits well above historical averages."

MISCONCEPTION #1:
BONDS ARE SAFE EVEN WHEN INTEREST RATES RISE

FINRA Bond Alert	// Potential Change in Bond Values (Bond Duration Years)									
What will happen to bond values if interest rates rise by 1%?		2	3	4	5	6	7	8	9	10
	+1%	-2%	-3%	-4%	-5%	-6%	-7%	-8%	-9%	-10%
	+2%	-4%	-6%	-8%	-10%	-12%	-14%	-16%	-18%	-20%
	+3%	-6%	-9%	-12%	-15%	-18%	-21%	-24%	-27%	-30%
	+4%	-8%	-12%	-16%	-20%	-24%	-28%	-32%	-36%	-40%
	+5%	-10%	-15%	-20%	-25%	-30%	-35%	-40%	-45%	-50%

As you know, one of my biggest concerns is the possibility of rising interest rates. If interest rates rise even a few percentage points, the deficit will soar. Brian Reidl, a budget expert at the libertarian-leaning Manhattan Institute, said, "While Congress must focus on addressing the pandemic and recession, the projected doubling of the national debt through 2030 should scare taxpayers."

It is problematic. A family, city, county, state or federal government cannot continue to spend more than the revenue it creates. The buck has to stop somewhere.

So, where does "It depends" come into play?

We are all facing a new normal that may last another six months or several years. COVID-19 should be likened to the changes we saw in our lives after 9/11. "Things" will never be the same.

And, so it is with our retirement plans: *things will never be the same.* We could see extreme volatility in the markets over the next several years. In these times, and if you are in or near retirement, you must make adjustments to make sure your boat can safely navigate the choppy and dangerous waters ahead.

When a family asks me a question about what is the best investment, I often respond, "It depends." And, it depends on so very much. Some decisions people make are emotional and some are very rational. Are you having to build a fund for retirement? Do you want to create predictable income? Are you most concerned with your legacy or are you more philanthropically inclined? How can we help you to accelerate the impact of your wealth?

No one has a crystal ball and no one can tell you how to time the markets or what the Fed might do next. We are in unprecedented and challenging times, and unless we have a carefully constructed plan to weather the storms ahead, able to move quickly and decisively, the next 10 to 20 years of retirement will not be the golden ones we have visualized and not the vision that Madison Avenue has sold us.

My primary and most important advice to any family or business trying to navigate the waters of retirement is make sure your assets are non-correlated. And, by that I don't just mean you have different stocks and bonds or a potpourri of mutual funds and ETFs. There are some truly non-correlated funds that you should explore and make a part of your plan.

Resources
First, find a true fiduciary who has your best interest in the recommendations he/she makes, and hold their feet to the fire.

Get educated.

There has never been a better time to become educated on the vital decisions you will have to make in the next 20 years. Do it now. Due to this public health crisis, there are more online courses, Zoom meetings and ways to remotely learn than we could have ever imagined in the recent past. Information is at the tips of your fingers (or keyboard) and it is yours to harvest.

At my firm, we have filmed a number of "ED Talks" on financial education. There are 15 videos available on demand on our website. In those, we cover Replacing the Bond Position in Your Portfolio, Fixed Index Annuities, The Role of a Fiduciary, Live, Quit or Die – Long Term Care Solutions, and more.

We have also created LionsGate Advisors University where you can take a virtual class on many of the ideas I have introduced in this book. These courses are offered on demand with great white papers to back up the strategies.

Several semesters a year, I teach these classes (now virtually all via Zoom) at several community colleges and at the University of Missouri at Osher Lifelong Learning Institute, which offers classes in financial education as well as many other interesting subjects. Go to their website at www. https://extension2.missouri.edu/programs/sher-lifelong-learning-institute and get familiar with the offerings. Set your ship on a course to learn. Sign up and empower yourself.

We have over 100 podcasts available on our website at Lions-Gate hosted by Jonathan Krueger and Mark Ralf, called "Living a Richer Life by Design". You can find it via Apple Podcast, or wherever you get your podcasts.

Applied knowledge is POWER!

Listen, listen, learn, learn. In these times, there are not many excuses for not taking advantage of these and other resources to learn and grow.

Our website is www.lionsgateadvisors.com. Go to the Educational Resources to begin your journey.

To you, my readers and families on your retirement journey, let me say what an honor it is to know you have read my words and ideas.

What will your retirement journey look like?

It depends. My nephew and niece, ages 32 & 37, both just retired from Amazon. My nephew and his wife are on a very specialized journey for retirement that will take them on unimaginable trips to work to make the planet a better place to live for us all. Their plan will be different from the 65-year-old who has just retired. Both my nephew and niece must plan for 50-60 years, so, their plans will be different from each others, as yours will be from your friends and neighbors. It depends.

LionsGate Advisors was founded on the premise that we cannot be all things to all people, but rather all things to a select few. We are on a mission to help people truly understand their finances with no mumbo-jumbo or computer programs spitting out a plan. For you, this book is written with love, another word that has meanings in Greek that are much more vibrant than they are in English. I share with you the LionsGate Advisors retirement strategies with Agape love—love expecting nothing in return but that you find peace and security in your work and retirement.

If life were predictable it would cease to be life, and be without flavor. -Eleanor Roosevelt

---

The Lion's Roar:
Key Takeaways from Chapter 17
- Especially in the post-COVID world, investors must be willing to adapt as the market (and its impact on your portfolio) shifts.

- Consult a true fiduciary for help. Their unbiased advice will chart a straight course.
- Make sure your portfolio is filled with truly non-correlated assets.
- Enjoy your life and retirement. We get only one chance, there are no do-overs. Listen, listen, love, love.

FUNDING LIFE INSURANCE AS A CONTINGENT ASSET CLASS IN A BALANCED PORTFOLIO

BY JONATHAN KRUEGER

Life insurance is often viewed as a product of necessity to provide liquidity to meet estate, personal and business obligations. Little to no thought is given to life insurance as a contingent asset class whose often sizeable death benefit impacts an investment portfolio and affects other asset classes. "In the mind of some clients, there is often an indirect connection between their life insurance and their other investments," says Douglas A. Copeland, a principal in the St. Louis-based law firm of Copeland, Thompson, Jeep, PC. Douglas, an estate planning attorney and a past president of the Missouri Bar Association, recognizes when someone owns a life insurance policy with a significant death benefit, this knowledge sometimes impacts their investment decisions. "Their risk tolerance rises with their non-insurance investments because they know there is a pot of money to mitigate any losses in the form of policy death benefit."

Showing a formal relationship between life insurance and other assets can shape investment behavior. When investment managers and estate planners analyze life insurance similarly to how they review other investments such as bonds, stocks and private equity, the influential role life insurance plays in a well-performing investment strategy is evident.

Expected Return

The traditional positioning of life insurance by the investment community tends to only consider the expected return realized on the income-tax-free death benefit when it is paid. This is computed by measuring the return of the death benefit against the premiums paid over time. Generally, at life expectancy, most clients will realize a return from a permanent type of life insurance, such as whole life or universal life, of between 5% and 7%. This is a decent return in the middle of the returns expected from private equity and government bonds.

An investment manager utilizing life insurance as a contingent asset class will find this traditional method incomplete, and will want to take two additional steps for a complete asset class analysis as laid out by economists Harry Markowitz and William F. Sharpe. First, in a 1952 essay, Markowitz unveiled his Modern Portfolio Theory where he theorized that, in addition to determining an expected return, individual portfolio assets should also be analyzed for their expected risk, which is the risk of not achieving the expected return.

Then, in 1966, Sharpe developed what is now known as the Sharpe Ratio. The final step to complete an asset class analysis relies upon the Sharpe Ratio to measure the performance of an investment, such as a real estate investment or security in a portfolio, compared to a risk-free asset, after adjusting for its risk. The

Sharpe Ratio characterizes how well the return of an asset compensates the investor for the risk taken, and is used to compare one asset against another in order to achieve the optimal portfolio based upon a client's tolerance.

Expected Risk

Computing the expected risk associated with obtaining the expected return from life insurance is measured by standard deviation, which is the average amount by which returns over a specific time vary from the mean. Specifically, death benefit deviation is the average amount by which the projected return on investments ("ROIs"), adjusted for their probability of occurring, vary assuming death occurred in any year.

As they are contingent upon mortality and not the markets, each projected ROI is adjusted for and multiplied by the corresponding probability of surviving to and dying at each age. A standard deviation is calculated on these probability-weighted ROIs. The lower the standard deviation, the less risk there is of not obtaining the expected return. Standard deviations for life insurance among various ages, sex and health risks are commonly quite low, ranging from .15% to around 1.00%. Conversely, the standard deviation for other asset classes is significantly higher—over 4% for bonds and over 17% for stocks. Investment managers are able to visualize this risk-return for various asset classes by plotting them on a chart where the vertical axis is the expected return and the horizontal axis is the expected risk. This "efficient frontier" demonstrates the maximum return for a given risk or a minimum risk for a given return.

Sharpe Ratio

The final step in an asset class analysis is calculating the Sharpe Ratio, the average return earned in excess of the risk-free rate per unit of volatility or total risk. Usually, any Sharpe ratio greater than 1.0 is considered acceptable to good by investors. A ratio higher than 2.0 is rated as very good. A ratio of 3.0 or higher is considered excellent.

The formula for the Sharpe Ratio subtracts the risk-free rate from the expected return of the portfolio and then divides the result by the standard deviation of the portfolio's expected risk. The risk-free rate represents the interest an investor would expect from an absolutely risk-free investment over a specified period of time, such as cash or U.S. government bonds.

For example, cash is expected to grow at roughly 2.1% annually over the next 25 years. If the expected return from life insurance is 6% and the standard deviation is .40%, then the Sharpe Ratio is 9.75, an excellent rating. In comparison, Sharpe Ratios for most other asset classes are commonly found to be under .50 and, on their own, not considered good risks.

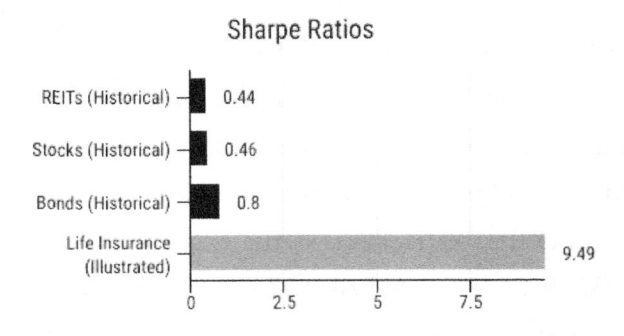

Sharpe Ratios

REITs (Historical)	0.44
Stocks (Historical)	0.46
Bonds (Historical)	0.8
Life Insurance (Illustrated)	9.49

Balancing a Portfolio

Armed with Sharpe Ratios for various asset classes, investment managers are able to mix a number of asset classes to achieve a blended Sharpe Ratio which matches the expectations for return and risk. When an investor is expecting that a significant sum of death benefit and life insurance has a high Sharpe Ratio, life insurance is the ideal contingent asset class to use as a foundation for mixing in other investments.

An investment manager may use the low risk of life insurance's expected return to hedge against riskier asset classes such as REITs or foreign equities. In practice, life insurance is used to reduce risk and increase risk-adjusted return in a portfolio, which is especially desired for portfolios held for wealth transfer.

Funding Life Insurance

The decision to purchase life insurance usually comes long after a portfolio has been established. As a result, obtaining the liquidity to pay premiums can be challenging and end up doing more damage than good for a portfolio's integrity and performance. Usually the portfolio itself is looked at for possible sources of premiums. Is there the ability to draw down fixed assets over time or can capital gains assets be liquidated with little to no unrealized gains? If so, can the same strategies be counted on to provide the cash to pay each premium installment?

One solution might be to leverage some of the investments in the portfolio to provide liquidity. Placing indebtedness on existing asset classes, if possible, has a slew of negative implications for a portfolio's risk and return and reduces the positive impact of the life insurance policy on the portfolio. A more efficient and less impactful method for applying leverage is to obtain lending against the cash value of the life insurance policy.

"Whether someone needs life insurance for its death benefit or to use a policy's cash value for future liquidity, it can sometimes make sense to use debt to purchase cash value life insurance," says Paul D. Larson, CFP®, CLU, the Founder of Larson Financial Group, a national financial planning firm headquartered in the St. Louis area. "Premium financing involves arbitrage where a client will evaluate the cost of debt versus return. Today's low lending interest rate can make this strategy attractive."

Premium financing is a way for qualified buyers to use third-party financing to pay for sizeable life insurance premiums with minimal initial and ongoing cash flow. A one-time or series of loans is typically obtained from a lender who may be willing to loan the entire premium, utilizing the policy cash value as collateral. Lenders will often credit the cash value between 90% and 100% for the first form of collateral and, in some situations, loans are made where the policy is pledged as the only collateral. Loan rates range from one-month to 12-month LIBOR plus 100 to 250 basis points.

The loan is usually paid back from the policy's cash value at a point in the future—usually after 10 years or more—or paid back at death from the policy's death benefit. In the meantime, the client's other portfolio investments remain untouched and positioned and performing as the investment manager designed.

Michael J. Silver, a partner in the St. Louis office of law firm Husch Blackwell, LLP, encourages clients to fully understand the economics of financing the premium for a life insurance policy. "Illustrations are only as accurate as the assumptions used to create them and actual performance may begin to deviate from the illustrations as early as the first day a policy is in force," says Silver, whose practice focuses on financial services and private wealth. "Those considering premium financing should ask for illustrative models which stress test performance of the strategy. This is where uncertain aspects such as interest rates and current policy assumptions are varied to understand the outcome."

Speaking the Same Language
A life insurance policy's death benefit has a meaningful impact on a client's wealth and should be positioned as such. The investment manager is able to apply the criteria and methodology of Modern Portfolio Theory to life insurance and position life insurance in the same manner as other asset classes. It is important to note policy ownership and premium funding considerations must be addressed in respect of any estate or gift tax planning concerns. Clients should seek guidance from a tax, legal or investment professional accordingly.

Life Insurance Funding with Premium Financing
After recognizing the benefits of life insurance to your overall financial health, the next step is figuring out the most efficient way to pay for a policy. While the obvious option may be paying from cash on-hand, this can be problematic where you have liquidity challenges and your funds are committed elsewhere or you simply need your money for living expenses. Moreover, if you are paying

your policy premium annually, this will be a recurring dilemma. The solution may be premium loan financing.

When seeking moderate-to-large sums of life insurance, affluent individuals are increasingly asking about premium-financed life insurance in order to acquire the amount of insurance they need while limiting their out-of-pocket costs. This financing permits clients to maintain flexibility in their cash flow and to keep capital deployed in higher yielding assets without having to liquidate those assets to pay for the policy.

The Arrangement

Financing premiums is a way for qualified borrowers to use third-party financing to pay for sizeable life insurance premiums with minimal initial and ongoing cash flow. Clients can benefit from potential arbitrage between the growth in cash value in the insurance policy versus the interest due on the loan each year. Here is how it works.

A one-time or a series of loans is typically obtained from either a bank with which a client has an established relationship or from a lender which has a focus in financing life insurance premiums. Lenders generally loan the entire premium amount, utilizing the policy cash value as collateral, and usually credit the cash value between 90% and 100% as the first form of collateral. In some situations, loans are made where the policy is pledged as the only collateral. Loan rates range from one-month to 12-month LIBOR plus 100 to 250 basis points, with relationship banks more apt to offer more favorable loan terms and interest rates.

The loan is usually paid back from the policy's cash value at a point in the future—generally after 10 or more years—or paid back at death from the policy's proceeds. The loan could also be paid back at the surrender of the policy or with other assets. In the meantime, the client's capital remains positioned elsewhere, earning a rate likely far higher than that of the life insurance policy.

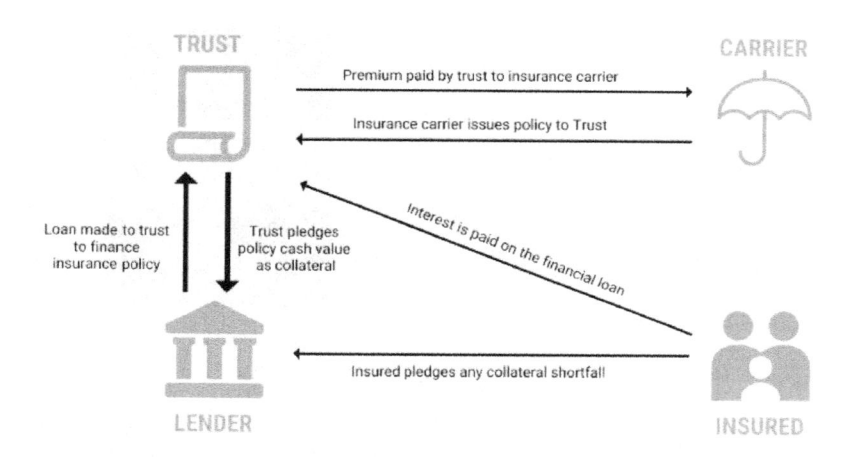

```
         TRUST                                                    CARRIER
                    Premium paid by trust to insurance carrier
                  ─────────────────────────────────────────→
                    Insurance carrier issues policy to Trust
                  ←─────────────────────────────────────────

                                    Interest is paid on the financial loan
 Loan made to trust     Trust pledges
    to finance          policy cash value
 insurance policy       as collateral


                    Insured pledges any collateral shortfall
                  ←─────────────────────────────────────────
         LENDER                                                   INSURED
```

Qualifying

Obtaining financing for life insurance premiums is not for everyone and, like any transaction involving a lender, you must qualify. At minimum, you should expect to have a net worth of at least $3 million and an annual income of more than $500,000.

Such minimums usually apply when the client intends to purchase a smaller amount of insurance and to use the policy to accumulate cash value growth to supplement future income, rather than purchasing a large policy for estate tax liabilities or to position within a portfolio as a contingent asset class. In the latter scenario, a client should be prepared to demonstrate a net worth in excess of $5 million and an annual income of more than $1 million to qualify for premium financing.

Financial Qualifications

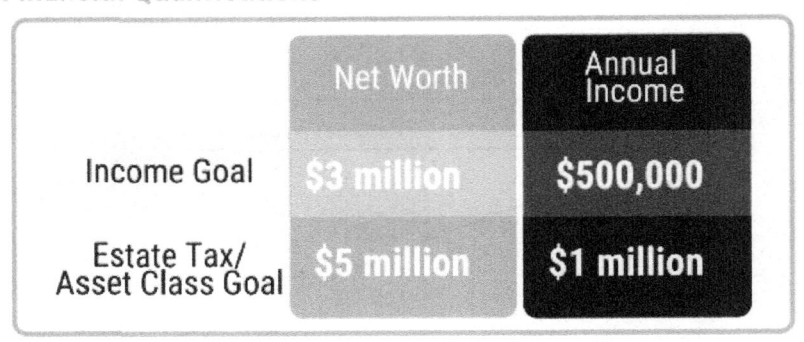

	Net Worth	Annual Income
Income Goal	$3 million	$500,000
Estate Tax/ Asset Class Goal	$5 million	$1 million

Life insurance companies will have additional requirements to meet before these carriers will permit their policies to be sold under a premium finance arrangement. These requirements are intended to increase the likelihood financed policies will remain in force and not fail in the first few years. Such conditions are in addition to the standard insurability justifications, which include proving an insurance need and demonstrating a level of wealth where a policy's proceeds will not "enrich" the policyholder.

Many life insurers will ask applicants to show proof that the first premium can be paid from cash on hand. In other words, in order to obtain a loan for the first premium, an applicant will need to show evidence of having the same amount of the loan in a liquid position. Next, particularly in situations where more premium is paid to lessen the number of years of premium payments, life insurers might require an applicant to prove they have the liquidity to make premium payments annually should lending be unavailable.

For example, without financing, the annual premium payment for a policy is $500,000 for the life of the insured. A financing arrangement might require just 10 annual premium payments, but of a higher amount of $1,500,000 to obtain the same result as the annual payment schedule. In this scenario, a lender might require the applicant to prove they have $1,500,000—the amount of the first loan—in cash, as well as having, through savings or income not needed for living expenses, $500,000 in cash each year in case a loan cannot be obtained to pay the premium.

Risks

There are several risks to consider before moving forward with a premium financing transaction and these risks generally fall into three categories:

Personal Risks are largely related to someone's net worth, liquidity and posted collateral. If, for example, net worth fell or the collateral was insufficient or moved so it was improperly held, it may be difficult to obtain future premium loans or the outstanding loan could be called.

Lending Risks are almost always associated with the interest rates for loans but may also come from changes to other terms. For instance, a change in loan duration or in repayment terms can make a premium loan less desirable.

Policy Risks involve changes to the performance of the life insurance policy. While a policy can perform better than predicted, it can also fail to meet expectations with regards to its crediting rate or dividend payments.

Service and Review

Perhaps the most effective action you can take to mitigate the impact of these risks is to engage a professional financial advisor who reviews your policy, your personal situation and your financing structure every six months. Adjustments can then be made to keep your plan on track and lessen the impact of external events.

Do not worry if you already purchased a life insurance policy and did not consider a lending arrangement. An often-overlooked opportunity for premium financing is with policies already in place. As loan interest rates have fallen dramatically over the last several years, it may make sense to re-evaluate your existing life insurance payment strategy. You could end up not having to make annual premium payments to your policy and, instead, make lower-cost interest payments to a lender for financing.

Ownership

Life insurance policies purchased through premium financing often have sizable death benefits and attention should be given to how these policies are owned. If the deceased insured owned the policy on the date of death, the whole amount of the death benefit is included in the estate and subject to estate tax. Although there is currently a generous estate tax exemption of $11,850,00 per person (2020), this is scheduled to sunset at the end of 2025 to just over $5,000,000. In addition, Congress and the president could act to change these amounts at any time.

Most purchasers of large life insurance policies will purchase them outside of their estates where the policy is held by an irrevocable life insurance trust (ILIT). The ILIT is both the owner and the beneficiary of the policy and receives the death benefit income-tax free at the death of the insured in order to distribute to trust beneficiaries.

If the intent of the policy is as a contingent asset class, consideration should be given to how the policy's death benefit will fit with other portfolio assets and how the entire portfolio can be accessed during lifetime or efficiently transferred at death to heirs.

Premium financing can be a powerful tool to help purchase life insurance while saving money by protecting liquidity that is best deployed elsewhere. The strategy is complex, and any plan design should take into account your risk tolerance and access to capital.

APPENDIX

Reference chart page 103

KEY ASSUMPTIONS:

Average Inflation 2.5%
Sequence of Returns Risk
Monte Carlo Analysis

RISK CONTINUUM

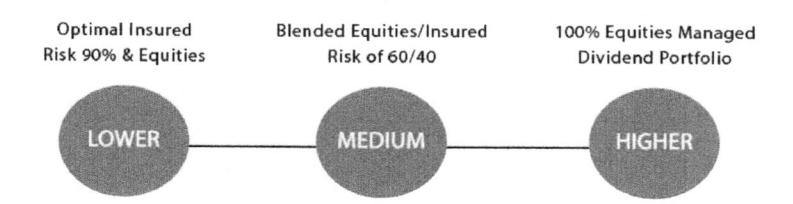

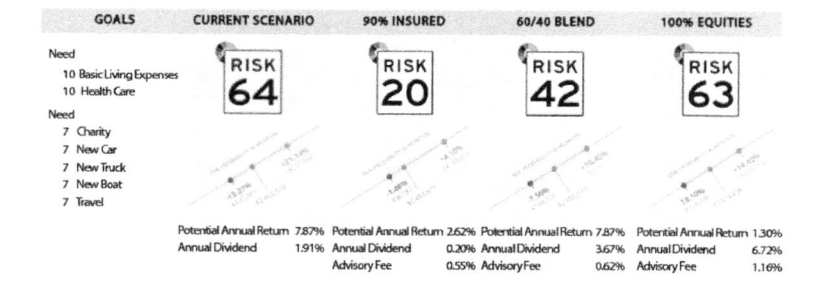

Optimal Insured Risk 90% & Equities	Blended Equities/Insured Risk of 60/40	100% Equities Managed Dividend Portfolio
LOWER	MEDIUM	HIGHER

GOALS	CURRENT SCENARIO	90% INSURED	60/40 BLEND	100% EQUITIES
Need	RISK **64**	RISK **20**	RISK **42**	RISK **63**
10 Basic Living Expenses				
10 Health Care				
Need				
7 Charity				
7 New Car				
7 New Truck				
7 New Boat				
7 Travel				
	Potential Annual Return 7.87%	Potential Annual Return 2.62%	Potential Annual Return 7.87%	Potential Annual Return 1.30%
	Annual Dividend 1.91%	Annual Dividend 0.20%	Annual Dividend 3.67%	Annual Dividend 6.72%
		Advisory Fee 0.55%	Advisory Fee 0.62%	Advisory Fee 1.16%

THE SECURE ACT: WHAT DOES IT MEAN FOR YOU?

The SECURE Act was passed at the end of 2019, with most provisions going into effect on January 1, 2020. It can be confusing to wade through the legislation and extract the implications of these changes. Now, more than ever, working with a financial professional is key to determining whether the SECURE Act could change your financial strategy going forward. Meanwhile, for an overview of what to expect from this new legislation, read on.

Explaining the SECURE Act

"SECURE" stands for "Setting Every Community Up for Retirement." The bill is intended to provide additional incentives to help people save more for retirement over a longer period of time, among other changes. The ideas behind the SECURE Act had been worked on for years before they were folded into a broader spending bill in late 2019. The bill passed on December 20, 2019, 13 years after the Pension Protection Act of 2006, the last time such dynamic changes were made.[1]

Changes to Retirement Accounts

The most sweeping and widely discussed changes brought about by the SECURE Act were how retirement accounts were affected.

These changes included changing the age for taking Required Minimum Distributions (RMDs), which may allow for some individuals to continue saving for retirement over a longer period of time. However, financial strategies, like Stretch IRAs, were also affected. We'll explore these in more detail below.[2]

Limits on Stretch IRAs

The legislation "modifies" the Required Minimum Distribution rules in regard to defined contribution plans and Individual Retirement Account (IRA) balances upon the death of the account owner. Under the new rules, distributions to non-spouse beneficiaries are generally required to be distributed by the end of the 10th calendar year following the year of the account owner's death.[3]

It's important to highlight that the new rule does not require the non-spouse beneficiary to take withdrawals during the 10-year period. But all the money must be withdrawn by the end of the 10th calendar year following the inheritance.

A surviving spouse of the IRA owner, disabled or chronically ill individuals, individuals who are not more than 10 years younger than the IRA owner, and children of the IRA owner who have not reached the age of majority may have other minimum distribution requirements.

Let's say that a person has a hypothetical $1 million IRA. Under the new law, their non-spouse beneficiary may want to consider taking at least $100,000 a year for 10 years regardless of their age. For example, say you are leaving your IRA to a 50-year-old child. They must take all the money from the IRA by the time they reach age 61. Before the rule change, a 50-year-old child could "stretch" the money over their expected lifetime, or roughly, 30 more years.

IRA Contributions and Distributions

Another major change is the removal of the age limit for traditional IRA contributions. Before the SECURE Act, you were required to stop making contributions at age 70-½. Now, you can continue to make contributions as long as you meet the earned-income requirement.[4]

Also, as part of the Act, you are mandated to begin taking required minimum distributions (RMDs) from a traditional IRA at age 72, an increase from the prior age of 70-½. Allowing money to remain in a tax-deferred account for an additional 18 months (before needing to take an RMD) may alter some previous projections of your retirement income.[4]

The SECURE Act's rule change for RMDs only affects Americans turning 70-½ in 2020 and beyond. For these taxpayers, RMDs will become mandatory at age 72. If you meet this criterion, your first RMD won't be necessary until April 1 after your 72nd birthday.[4]

Conduit Trusts

Before the SECURE Act, a Conduit Trust was an easier way to safeguard the life of an inherited IRA. Instead of making an individual the beneficiary of the IRA, the trust would become the beneficiary. If you were concerned about how your heirs might spend their inheritance, putting your IRA into a conduit trust was one approach to help manage distributions.[5]

Under the SECURE Act, if the beneficiary of a conduit trust does not qualify as an eligible designated beneficiary (EDB), then the entire plan balance is required to be distributed by the 10th anniversary of the plan holder's death. The end result of this is that the previous benefits of the conduit trust might be limited to the new 10-year rule.[5]

Keep in mind, a trust involves a complex set of tax rules and regulations. Before moving forward with a conduit trust or any other trust, you'd be wise to work with a professional who is familiar with these rules and regulations.[6]

Annuities

This might be the most complicated part of the SECURE Act. It's now easier for your employer-sponsored retirement plans to have annuities added to their investment portfolio. This was accomplished by reducing the fiduciary responsibilities that a company may incur in the event the annuity provider goes bankrupt. The benefit is that annuities may provide retirees with guaranteed lifetime income. The downside, however, is that annuities are often the incorrect vehicle for investors who are just starting out or far from retirement age.[7]

Businesses

In terms of wide-ranging potential, the SECURE Act may offer its biggest change in the realm of multi-employer retirement plans. Previously, multiple-employer plans were only open to employers within the same field or ones that shared some other "common characteristics." Now, small businesses have the opportunity to buy into larger plans alongside other small businesses, without the prior limitations. This opens small businesses to a much wider field of options.[8]

Another big change for small-business employer plans comes for part-time employees. Before the SECURE Act, these retirement plans were not offered to employees who worked fewer than 1,000 hours in a year. Now, the door is open for employees who have either worked 1,000 hours in the space of one full year or to those who have worked at least 500 hours per year for three consecutive years.[9]

College Students

For those who have graduate funding, the SECURE Act allows students to use a portion of their income to start investing in retirement savings. The SECURE Act also contains a clause to include "aid in the pursuit of graduate or postdoctoral study." A grant or fellowship would be considered income that the student could invest into a retirement vehicle.[10]

One other provision of the SECURE Act: you can use your 529 Savings Plan to pay for up to $10,000 of student debt. Money in a 529 Plan can also be used to pay for costs associated with an apprenticeship.[11]

Changes for Families

Are you having a baby or adopting? Under the SECURE Act, you can withdraw up to $5,000 per individual, tax free, from your IRA to help cover costs associated with a birth or adoption. However, there are stipulations. The money must be withdrawn within the first year of this life change. Otherwise, you may be open to the tax penalty.[12]

Conclusions

The SECURE Act changed the landscape of retirement savings and may necessitate changes to your financial strategy. Let's work together to make sure that you are optimizing what's available and taking full advantage of the new rules. As always, you are welcome to reach out with any questions.

FOOTNOTES FOR THE SECURE ACT

1. Forbes, January 10, 2020.
2. WaysAndMeans.House.gov, April 2, 2019.
3. Forbes, December 29, 2019.
4. JD Supra, December 23, 2019.
5. WaysAndMeans.House.gov, 2019.
6. MarketWatch, January 9, 2020.
7. MarketWatch, January 16, 2020. The guarantees of an annuity contract depend on the issuing company's claims-paying ability. Annuities have contract limitations, fees, and charges, including account and administrative fees, underlying investment management fees, mortality and expense fees, and charges for optional benefits. Most annuities have surrender fees that are usually highest if you take out the money during the initial years of the annuity contact. Withdrawals and income payments are taxed as ordinary income. If a withdrawal is made prior to age 59-½, a 10% federal income tax penalty may apply (unless an exception applies).
8. WaysAndMeans.House.gov, 2019.
9. MarketWatch, December 21, 2019.
10. Forbes.com, December 23, 2019. A 529 plan is a college savings plan that allows individuals to save for college on a tax-advantaged basis. State tax treatment of 529 plans is only one factor to consider prior to committing to a savings plan. Also, consider the fees and

expenses associated with the particular plan. Whether a state tax deduction is available will depend on your state of residence. State tax laws and treatment may vary. State tax laws may be different than federal tax laws. Earnings on nonqualified distributions will be subject to income tax and a 10% federal tax penalty.

11. Forbes, December 23, 2019.

12. Congress.gov, May 23, 2019. For a comprehensive review of your personal situation, always consult with a tax or legal advisor. Neither the named broker-dealer nor any of its representatives may give legal or tax advice.

DISCLOSURE

Investment advisory services offered through Lion Street Advisors, a SEC Registered Investment Advisor, and Insurance products and services are offered through LionsGate Advisors.

Information current as of March 29, 2020.

Opinions, estimates, forecasts, and statements of financial market trends that are based on current market conditions constitute our judgment and are subject to change without notice.

This material is for information purposes only and is not intended as an offer or solicitation with respect to the purchase or sale of any security.

Investing involves risk, including the potential loss of principal. No investment strategy can guarantee a profit or protect against loss in periods of declining values.

The Standard & Poor's 500 Index is a capitalization-weighted index of 500 stocks designed to measure performance of the broad domestic economy through changes in the aggregate market value of 500 stocks representing all major industries.

All indexes are unmanaged and cannot be invested into directly.

Opinions expressed are not intended as investment advice or to predict future performance. Past performance does not guarantee future results.

Consult your financial professional before making any investment decision.

All information is believed to be from reliable sources; however, we make no representation as to its completeness or accuracy. Please consult your financial professional for further information.

These are the views of Platinum Advisor Marketing Strategies, LLC, and not necessarily those of the named representative, broker/dealer or investment advisor and should not be construed as investment advice.